C R U X

THE PLACE OF THE CROSS
IN THE PROCESS OF TRANSFORMATION

DAVE ANDREWS

MOSAIC PRESS

Published in Australia by
Mosaic Press
508 High St
Preston Vic. 3072
Australia

Mosaic Press is an imprint of Mosaic Resources Pty Ltd

ISBN 9781743241080

All scripture quotations are taken from the NIV.

First published 2013

Cataloguing-in-Publication entry is available for the National Library of Australia
http:/catalogue.nla.gov.au/.

Book design by John Healy
Printed by Openbook Howden

For TEAR Australia and TEAR's partners
in MICAH Network and MICAH Challenge.

'God sent his "only beloved Son" into the world to die *"for us"*; but the story d(oes) not make it at all clear what "for" meant.'

A. S. Byatt [1]

'No doctrine…can represent the fullness of Christian tradition which does not explain how the world is made better by the cross.'

H.E. Turner [2]

'The church has never had any official doctrine of the atonement. The church has left every(one) to find (their) own way to salvation through the life and death of Jesus.'

William Barclay [3]

'It is my view, that the cross - and the unique critique, charisma, and catalyst that it provides - is the crux of the struggle for any genuine personal, social, and political change.'

Dave Andrews

Notes

1   A. S. Byatt *The God I Want* p73

2   H.E. Turner *The Patristic Doctrine Of Redemption* p46

3   W Barclay *Crucified and Crowned* SCM London 1961 p95

Contents

Foreword. 9

Preface 11

A Place For A Story. . . . . : 13

"The Cross As Critique". 19

"The Cross As Charisma" 45

"The Cross As Catalyst". 71

FOREWORD

Dave Andrews has long been a voice of passion, grace and truth for those who seek to follow the radical way of the cross of Christ. These provocative essays exploring the story of the cross ought to become a highlight of his already brilliant writings. In them Dave forces us to confront our propensity to distort the cross, making it into the very same kind of violent myth it seeks to subvert.

How we understand the cross forms the very centre of how we answer questions regarding what it means to be God's people—who are we, what are we to do, and how are we to do it? Dave offers us an alternative to contemporary violent atonement theories by showing that the cross, far from asserting violent power, unmasks it, puts it on public display! With his characteristic sensitivity, Dave shows us that the problems inherent in the narrative of the cross lie not with the cross itself, but with our telling of the story, with our understanding of that crescendo of history.

Discussion of the atonement is of course fashionable in the Western Church in recent times, and so Dave's subject matter is not unprecedented. However his approach is refreshing. Dave manages to communicate difficult concepts, typically argued in scholarly contexts, in language that is accessible for all people. What he has written is a fantastic starting point for those who are exploring these themes for the first time as well as a stimulating read for those more experienced.

In addition to Dave's well-reasoned arguments are his wonderful stories that emanate from a life of trying to embody what he teaches. Dave's persuasive power goes beyond the mere cerebral as he shares both personal and anecdotal tales of cross-centred love. These stories put 'flesh on the bones' of the theology Dave outlays, a theology of subversive ethics and incarnational love. Through such stories we are challenged and encouraged to more faithfully take up our own crosses and exhibit the costly grace and revolutionary compassion of Christ who suffered and died to save his people from their sins. Dave's liturgies, songs, poems and questions also provoke us into deep reflection and prayer, a response both appropriate and necessary.

I'm sure Dave's essays will prove controversial for some, simply because of the sensitive nature of the subject. However I wholeheartedly believe the challenge they pose to violent interpretations of Christ's redeeming work is a crucial one in the Church today. I wouldn't hesitate to recommend these essays to anyone questioning the meaning of the cross, those wanting to better understand the relevance of Jesus' death for kingdom mission today, or those who simply wish to be challenged and transformed by Jesus' revolutionary love.

Matthew Anslow,
National Young Adults Coordinator,
TEAR Australia 27/06/13

PREFACE

I first presented *Crux* as a series of papers, published in Zadok Perspectives, at a National Conference of TEAR Australia in Sydney. TEAR Australia is an Australian Christian aid agency committed to working with the poor in the light of the gospel.

For many years now I have been concerned that, though we as Christians often invoke Christ as the *reason* for our concern for our concern for the poor, seldom is there anything distinctively Christ-like about the *nature* of our concern for the poor.

In fact, in my experience, where the gospel has been referred to as framework for practice, it has often been reduced to a formula, that has not only underrated the value of work with the poor, but also undermined the faith of those working with the poor.

I have prepared these papers to help us reclaim the story of the cross, not as a *'formula'*, but as *'metanarrative'*, that can inspire our faith and inform the value of our work.

I know some of what I want to say will be considered to be quite controversial by the evangelical constituency from which I come. However, my intention is not to be controversial, but to be honest, and to simply raise critical issues about our understanding of the story of the cross, and how that understanding impacts on our work with the poor.

It is a great encouragement to me, amid the controversy surrounding the presentation of these papers, that respected evangelical leaders, like Tom Slater, the former National Director of the Australian Evangelical Alliance, have responded so enthusiastically.

In *Working Together*, Tom wrote: 'A recent highlight for me was the TEAR National Conference. Dave's input - three packed presentations on the cross - were riveting and deeply provocative. He strongly affirmed the centrality of the cross in our experience; at the same time challenging us to rethink some of (our) interpretative frameworks'.

'I readily admit', he conceded, 'to being disturbed at some points - but I welcome it. I was provoked in the best evangelical tradition, by having my nose well and truly rubbed in the scriptures - not isolated proof texts, but the broad sweep of both testaments...'

'These intelligent and passionate orations, includ(ing) memorable poetic liturgical prayer responses, were followed up by lengthy animated discussions. Contentious they may be, but I hope (these papers) will be available to a wider audience as soon as possible.'

When I presented these papers at the national conference, I did so with the disclaimer that: 'it should be noted that the views expressed in these papers are only those of the author, and do not necessarily reflect the views of either the board or the other staff of TEAR Australia'. That disclaimer still stands. For better, or worse, these are my views.

Dave Andrews
Brisbane 2013

A Place For A Story.

One of the biggest difficulties we face, in trying to figure out the place of the story of the cross in today's world, is that we live in a postmodern world, in which, it is said, there is no place at all for a *metastory* - like the story of the cross - anymore.

A *'metastory'*, or a *'metanarrative'*, is 'a big story that gives meaning to the smaller stories of our everyday lives'. We used to derive meaning from *metastories*, like the myth of progress, because these *metanarratives* gave us a reason to believe that, in the end, everything would be okay. However, over time, we discovered that many m*eta-stories* were self-serving *metanarratives* - manipulative, oppressive, and exploitative. So we were left with the suspicion that many of our favourite *metastories* were false.

Along with widespread skepticism about *metastories* in general, there is also a lot of cynicism about the story of the cross as a *metastory* in particular. 'What, after all, is the cross of Jesus Christ?' asks Joachim Kahl. Answering his own question, he poignantly replies: 'It is nothing but the sum total of a sado-masochistic glorification of pain!' [1]

Dorothee Soelle, the insightful writer of the classic book, *Suffering*, understands the outrage of critics like Joachim Kahl. She says that many theologians she knows have told the story of the cross in a way that, in the final analysis, has amounted to ' nothing but the sum total of a sado-masochistic glorification of pain.' And that, she declares, included her famous compatriot Jurgen Moltmann, the well-known author of a much-loved masterpiece on the story of the cross.

Soelle points out that in *The Crucified God* Moltmann depicted Jesus on the cross as 'suffering at the hands of God'[2]. Which, she argues, amounted to an understanding of suffering as a process in which one member of the community of God masochistically endures the excruciating pain that another member of the community of God sadistically inflicts on him'. [3]

Soelle asks: 'Who wants such a God? A theology that is developed from this starting point will end up worshipping the executioner.'[4] And 'worshipping the executioner', in one way or another, is exactly what many Christians have done - with devastating consequences. Millions of innocent men, women, and children, have been tortured and slaughtered. If you don't believe me, just ask a Holocaust survivor or Rwandan refugee!

Where can we go from here?

On the one hand, we know we need a *metanarrative*. Without a *metastory* we are left with a collection of disconnected stories, but with no larger story that we can use to put our little stories together. Only a *metanarrative* can provide a framework of on which we can weave the unifying fabric of community from the diverse threads that are our lives.

On the other hand, the *metanarrative* we hold dear has seemingly failed to provide the *metastory* we need. Instead of creating unity in diversity, the story of the cross has often been used to rationalize ethnic cleansing and justify genocide again and again.

Where we go from here with the story of the cross depends on whether we see the problems with it as *intrinsic*, or *extrinsic*. If you see the problems as *intrinsic* to the story - in the very nature of the story itself - you have to discard the story of the cross as a useful *metastory* once and for all. But if you see the problems not as *intrinsic*, but as *extrinsic* - not in the nature of the story, but in the manner in which it has been told - then what you have to discard is the telling of the story, rather than the story itself.

I, for one, see the problems associated with the story of the cross as problems that are associated with the manner in which the story has been told, rather than with the nature of the story itself.

I don't think we need to look for a new story. But we do need to look for a new way of telling of the story. We need to find a new way of telling the 'old, old story'; which rescues it from its terminal association with sado-masochism; and restores it to its true position as 'the greatest love story ever told'. Then, and only then, will the story of the cross be able to take its place as the *metastory* we need to help us with the process of deconstructing and reconstructing our postmodern world.

The irrepressible religious broadcaster, Tom Wright, says, 'It would be silly to claim Jesus as the first great postmodernist, but the grain of truth in such a suggestion should be obvious. His actions were coded ways of deconstructing (his world). Whatever Jesus was up to on Good Friday, it was not a covert power play. Violence, he insisted, could never be the way of bringing God's justice to the world. From the very beginning Christians have seen the crucifixion of Jesus as the greatest act of divine generosity.'[5]

This story challenges all other *metanarratives*. Not as 'one power play to another'. But as 'the subversion of all power plays'. Tragically, 'Christians have been constantly tempted to turn (the) message of love into a means of self-aggrandizement'. And 'then the story becomes the sort of *metanarrative* that postmodernity justifiably objects to'. But, in spite of the many times the gospel has been turned into propaganda, this story has managed to retain its integrity, and reassert its never-dominated, never-dominating quality, subverting 'the power plays' of those who try to co-opt it for their own purposes.

The story of the cross is a *metanarrative* that 'can never be deconstructed in the way that postmodernity has deconstructed the stories of modernism', because 'it is a story of love...risky and costly love...the self-giving love of God' - that is the very antithesis of all our modern self-serving *metanarratives.* [6]

The Story Of The Cross.

The story of the cross is the story of an unjust execution of an innocent man that took place in Palestine nearly 2000 years ago. It is full of great feeling, but it is told with immense emotional restraint. Yet the crucifixion of Jesus is narrated in manner that makes it unforgettable. And it has become the most widely told story in the world.

> *"And they brought (Jesus) to the place called Golgotha,*
> *which means 'the Place Of The Skull'.*
> *They offered him wine mixed with a drug called myrrh.*
> *But he would not drink it.*
> *Then they crucified him,*
> *and divided his clothes among themselves,*
> *Throwing dice to see*
> *who would get which piece of clothing.*
>
> *And the inscription of the charge against him read:*
> *'The King Of The Jews.'*
> *With ('The King') they also crucified two brigands;*
> *one on the right, and one on the left.*

And those who passed by ridiculed him,
shaking their heads, hurling insults at him.
'You saved others; but can you save yourself?'
'Let the Christ, come down from the cross,
that we may see and believe!'

And those crucified with him insulted him too.
At noon the whole country was covered with darkness,
which last for about three hours.
And at three o'clock Jesus cried out with a loud shout:
'Eloi, Eloi, lama sabachthani?' which means,
'My God, my God, why have you forsaken me?'
And some of the people who heard him said -
'Listen, he is calling for Elijah!'
And one ran up with a sponge soaked in cheap wine
and put it on the end of a stick.
Then he held it up to Jesus' lips and said, 'Wait!
Let us see whether Elijah will come to take him down.'
But when he had received the drink, Jesus cried out,
'It is finished! Father! Into your hands I place my spirit.'
He said this, then he died."[1]

The Meaning Of The Story.

Right from the very beginning the crucifixion meant different things to different people.

What people saw depended upon where they stood in relation to the execution. The cross meant one thing to the enemies of Jesus, another thing to the friends of Jesus, and something else altogether to Jesus himself.

The enemies of Jesus considered him to be 'one of those dangerous elements' in society that needed to be eliminated. To them he was: a 'heretical teacher' who undermined orthodox belief and behaviour; a 'false prophet' who predicted the total destruction of their beautiful temple; and a 'blasphemous fool' who went so far as to appropriate the prerogative of God - to forgive sin - for himself and his friends. For the enemies of Jesus, the cross was the appropriate comeuppance for an upstart. [2]

For the friends of Jesus, the cross was the final nail in the coffin of their faith. They considered him to be a 'good man', even a 'great man', perhaps even the 'Son of God'.

But the cross made them question every single thing that they ever believed about him. If he was such a 'good man' - such a 'great man' - how was it that he ended up being executed as criminal? Didn't the bible say 'anyone hanged on a tree is accursed?'[3] If he was 'such a blessing', how come he was cursed? He was supposed to be the 'Son of God'. But, if he was the 'Son of God', why did he feel so forsaken by the One he called his 'Father' that he cried out, 'My God, my God, why have you forsaken me?'[4]

For the friends of Jesus, the cross was the end of the road. To them, it was as if they had lost their way, forever. They didn't know which way to go anymore at all. But, for Jesus, himself, the cross *was* the way. The way forward, not only for him, but also for his friends. As far as Jesus was concerned, the cross was the way forward for all of us.

For Jesus, the cross came as no surprise. He had expected it. It was not an accident. But the consequence of the path he had chosen. He knew that to seek to be 'light',[5] in a world that 'loved darkness rather than light',[6] was going to be asking for trouble. And he told his friends he was more than willing to face it when the time came.[7] In fact, he told them, that the cross, when it came, would provide him with his best chance to fulfill his mission.[8] 'No one will take my life from me, I will give it, willingly, myself'.[9] 'A person can have no greater love than this - than to give their life for their friends.'[10]

But what was it Jesus was hoping to accomplish by giving his life for his friends? And what, if anything, has his death on the cross, 2000 years ago, got to do with us today?

These are the questions I want to try to answer over the course of the next few pages by re-examining the place of the story of the cross in the process of transformation.

For it is my view, that the cross, and the unique *critique, charisma,* and *catalyst* it equips us with, is at the crux of any struggle for genuine personal, social, and political change.

Notes

1 J. Kahl *The Misery Of Christianity* Cover
2 J.Moltmann *The Crucified God* SCM London 1979 p241ff
3 D. Soelle, Suffering, Fortress Philadelphia 1988 p27 ,
4 ibid p32, 29
5 T.Wright *The Myth Of The Millenium* Azure London 1999 pp73-74
6 Ibid p79

"The Cross As Critique".

*In the beginning was the Word, and the Word was with God
and the Word was God. Through him all things were made,
and without him nothing was made that has been made. In
him was life, and that life was the light of the world. He was
in the world, and though the world was made by him, the
world did not recognize him. He came to his own, but his
own did not receive him. The light sh(one) in the darkness
but the darkness did not understand it. This is the verdict:
Light has come into the world, but people love the darkness
rather than the light, because their deeds are evil. Everyone
who does evil hates the light because they do not want their
evil deeds to be exposed.   (John1: 1-10,3: 17-20)*

*Jesus said to them, 'Listen to another parable: There once
was a landowner who planted a vineyard, put a wall around
it, dug a hole for a winepress, and built a watchtower. Then
he rented out the vineyard to tenants and went away on a
journey. When the time came to gather the grapes he sent
his servants to the tenants to collect his fruit. The tenants
seized the servants; they beat one, then killed another, and
stoned another. Again the landowner sent other servants to
them, more than the first time, and the tenants treated them
the same way. Last of all he sent his son to them. "Surely
they will respect my son!" But when the tenants saw the son,
they said to themselves, "This is the owner's son. Come on
let's kill him, and his property will be ours!" So they seized
him, threw him out of the vineyard, and killed him.'
                              (Math. 21:33-39)*

*And as Jesus was going up to Jerusalem he took the twelve
disciples aside and spoke to them privately, as they walked
along. 'Listen', he told them, 'we are going up to Jerusalem,
where the Son of Man will be handed over to the chief priests
(of Israel) and the teachers of the Law. They will condemn him*

to death, then hand him over to the Gentiles who will mock him,
whip him, and crucify him.' (Math. 20:17-19)

And the chief priests (of Israel) stirred up the crowd...
'What will I do with the "King of the Jews"?' asked Pilate.
'Crucify him!' they shouted back.
'But what crime has he committed?' Pilate asked them.
'Crucify him! Crucify him!' they shouted all the louder.
Wanting to please the crowd...Pilate had Jesus flogged,
and handed him over to be crucified. (Mark15: 12-14)

(And) those who...were once enlightened...(who) abandon
their faith...are crucifying the Son of God all over again....
(Heb.6: 4-6)

For someone to die on a cross was not a very unusual story in first century Palestine. The Maccabean king, Jannaeus, crucified eight hundred leading Pharisees after an unsuccessful insurrection in 88 B.C.[11] The Roman general, Varus, crucified some two thousand insurgents in 4 B.C.[12] And the Roman general, Florus, crucified some three thousand six hundred more in A.D. 66.[13] While, during the final seige of Jerusalem in A.D.70, Titus is said to have ordered so many crucifixions that they ran out of wood for the crosses![14]

What made the death of Jesus unique, was not so much *how* he died, but *who* it was that died on the cross that day. As far as his disciples were concerned, the one who died on the cross that day was no ordinary man. To them, Jesus was the '*Christ*' - the '*Son of Man*' who was the '*Son of God*'[15]- the One who was '*with God*' and the One who '*was God*.'[16] So for them, when Jesus died on the cross that day, it wasn't just another death - it was the death of '*Life*' itself. The '*Light of Life*' itself was extinguished, and they found themselves engulfed by a terrible existential '*Darkness*', as the '*One they believed to be God almighty*' was ridiculed, tortured, and killed right in front of them.[17]

Now The Question Is - Who Killed Christ?

Some say: 'God!' After all, 'God is to blame for everything that goes down in the world.' Some even quote the scripture saying, God 'did not spare his own Son, but delivered him up for us all' (Romans 8:32). Some even go so far as to say, 'We must understand "delivered up" in its full sense, and not water it down to mean…"give". What happened here (on the cross) is what Abraham did not do to Isaac. (Abraham did not sacrifice Isaac. But God did sacrifice Christ.) He subjected Christ … to death.' [18] You may say to them, 'This is absurd. This wasn't suicide. This was murder. How could God possibly murder God?' No problems, they say. 'In the words of the dogma of the early church: the first person of the Trinity…(simply) annihilates the second….'[19] On the cross Christ is 'godforsaken' - literally 'forsaken by God'. Which is why he cries out in a loud voice:

'Eloi, Eloi, lama sabachthani?' - 'My God, my God, why have you forsaken me?' [20]

These views undergird the development of two often unrecognized, but often very influential schools of Christian theology - Christian *Sadism* and Christian *Masochism*.

Christian *Sadism* teaches that God is omnipotent and sends suffering to punish sin, and since we are all sinners, we can expect nothing but suffering. Jesus 'became sin, who knew no sin'[21] and was 'led like a lamb to the slaughter'[22]. Be warned: 'The Lord is fattening (sinners) for the slaughter!'.[23]

Christian *Masochism* teaches that God is omnipotent and sends suffering to make us repent from sin, so that the more we suffer, the better it is for us. Even Jesus had to 'learn obedience through the things that he suffered'[24]So, 'the very chastisements (the Lord) has inflicted upon us are just. Though (he) might inflict blows a hundredfold…we have merited them by our crimes.'[25]

The ideas taught by these schools of Christian theology have been behind some of the worst atrocities in Christian history. *Sadistic* Popes have callously called for crusades, saying, 'Cursed be the man who holds back his sword from the shedding of blood!' [26] And *Masochistic* Pastors have sycophantically comforted the families of victims, saying, 'The Lord giveth, and the Lord taketh away. Blessed be the name of the Lord!'[27]

And, the attitudes associated with these ideas are still very much with us even today.

Some time back a letter was sent to TEAR from a church in Queensland, complaining that TEAR was too preoccupied with issues like human rights. And as Steve Bradbury, the national director at that time, was due to visit Queensland soon, we thought it might be good to respond to this complaint by scheduling a meeting to discuss the issues face to face. So, at the appointed hour, Steve Bradbury, with a bit of moral support from Paul Mercer and myself, turned up for the meeting.

We were greeted at the door, and shown a chair at the end of a table, around which were seated a set of some of the most seriously dressed men I had ever seen. When we were all seated, a very somber looking man, at the head of the table, announced that he would select a passage from the bible to set the scene for our discussion. He picked up the big old book on the table in front of him, and, in a deep stentorian voice, began to read:

> *'In the cities of the nations,*
> *the Lord your God is giving you as an inheritance:*
> *Do not leave anything that breathes alive!*
> *Completely destroy them -*
> *the Hittites, the Amorites,*
> *the Canaanites, the Perizzites,*
> *the Hivites and the Jebusites -*
> *as the Lord your God has commanded you!'*[28]

Then, the somber man closed the book, and said, 'So you can see, that in the Bible there is no such thing as "inalienable human rights". God's people are simply called to do God's will' he said - with a cold, hard, matter-of-fact finality - *'whether that is to cure, or to kill!'*

I could hardly believe my ears. Here I was, in downtown Brisbane, the capital of peaceful sunny Queensland - 'beautiful one day, perfect the next' - and I was listening to a respected Christian leader still justifying wholesale slaughter in the name of God!

Now, it seems to me, that the *Sadism* and *Masochism* reflected in these statements are based on a distorted reading of the bible in general, and the story of the cross in partic-ular. Whether this distortion is deliberate, or not, is a matter for debate. But there are many *Sadists* and *Masochists* who have a vested interest in this distorted reading of the text. Because it projects the blame for suffering on to God, and thereby helps both the *Sadists* and the *Masochists* escape their responsibility for the suffering in the world.

If we read the story of the cross very carefully, it's very clear that God did not kill Christ.

God did 'not spare his Son' in the sense that He took the risk to send his Son into the world. [29] But, when He 'delivered' the Son of God to our doorstep as the Son of Man, He did so saying to himself, 'Surely they will respect my Son!'[30] However, when he came, 'his own people did not welcome him.'[31] He may have been 'the light of the world'. But they didn't want him. 'The people loved the darkness rather than the light; because their deeds were evil, and didn't want anybody to expose them.' [32] So they decided to get rid of him. And, as Jesus predicted, they eventually 'seized' him, and 'crucified' him. [33]

To say Jesus felt 'abandoned by everybody - including God', is quite different from saying that he 'blamed God' for his death. Nailed to that lonely wooden cross, his body wracked with pain, his soul broken with despair, there is no doubt Jesus felt utterly forsaken. And the question arose from deep inside him: 'My God, my God, why have you forsaken me?' But, to say Jesus 'felt forsaken', didn't mean that he 'was forsaken'. In fact, before the agony of crucifixion kicked in, Jesus himself had said, 'Don't you know I could call on my Father for help, and at once he could send me armies of angels?' [34] And when it was all over, Jesus turned to God, as the only One he felt he could trust, saying, 'Father into your safekeeping I commit my spirit.'[35]

It was *not* God who forsook Christ, but his disciples.[36] God was *not* the one who sold him for thirty pieces of silver - it was Judas.[37] God was *not* the one who denied him three times - it was Peter.[38] It was *not* God who killed Christ, but the powers that be, aided and abetted by the public.[39] God was *not* the one who stirred up the crowds - it was the chief priests.[40] God was *not* the one who cried, 'Crucify him! Crucify him!' - it was ordinary people, like you and me.[41] And, in the end, it was the authorities - a Jewish King and a Roman Governor - that nailed Christ to the cross. [42] *Not God!*

'So where was God when all this was happening?' you ask. Well, 'God was *in* Christ.' [43] God was *in* Christ - in his suffering. God was *in* Christ - in his forsakeness. He was not the perpetrator. He was not a spectator. He was *with the victim*, and He *was the victim*.

Jurgen Moltmann, (reacting to criticism of his views in *The Crucified God*,) states quite categorically that, '*The Father of Jesus is always on Jesus side - never on the side of the people who crucified him*'. [44] He quotes the scripture, saying: "*He who sees the Son sees the Father*"[45]. Then he goes on to say, 'in the suffering of the Son', is the suffering 'of the Father'. And he poignantly concludes, 'the Father suffers the death of the Son'.[46]

The Powers That Be And People Like You and Me.

When we read the story of the cross correctly, then we are confronted with the most profound and most terrifying critique of humanity in history. For we realize, to our horror, that it is not God who has killed Christ, but *the powers that be*, and *people like you and me*, who, in killing Christ, have killed God.

The powers that be are *the authorities* - the spiritual centres of traditions, institutions and systems of control that have immense power over our lives.[47] These cosmic forces, at the heart of our religious traditions, cultural institutions and governmental systems of law and order maintain their control over our lives through their claims to legitimacy. They claim they have 'a God-given right' to control because, they say, that as 'properly constituted authorities' they are the 'God-anointed, God-appointed guardians of our lives'.[48] And *people like you and me* are taught to submit ourselves to *the powers that be*, so that 'we can learn from God through them', as it says, in a lesson outline that was distributed in a religious instruction class at a local school some time back.[49]

However, in *Colossians*, Paul said Jesus 'made a pubic example' of *the powers that be*.[50] And, in his classic book on *Christ and the Powers*, Hendrik Berkhof explains just how Jesus made a public example - or public spectacle - of the Powers on the cross.

'It is precisely in the crucifixion that the true nature of the Powers has come to light. Now that the true God appears on earth in Christ, it becomes apparent that the Powers are inimical to him, not acting as His instruments but as His adversaries. The Scribes, representatives of the Jewish law, far from gratefully receiving Him who came in the name of the God of law, crucified him in the name of the temple. Pilate, representing Roman justice, shows what th(is) is worth when called upon to do justice to the truth Himself. (And) the Pharisees, personifying piety, crucified Him in the name of piety. Obviously "none of the rulers of this age', who let themselves be worshipped as divinities, understood God's wisdom, "for if they had known, they would not have crucified the Lord of glory."[51] Now they are unmasked as false gods by their encounter with Very God; they are "made a public spectacle".[52]

Walter Wink, in his three volume series on *Naming, Unmasking, and Engaging The Powers*, writes: 'Jesus died just like all the others who challenge the Powers that dominate the world. (But) some thing went awry (for the Powers) with Jesus. They scourged him with whips, but with each stroke of the lash their own illegitimacy was laid open. They stripped him naked and crucified him in humiliation, all unaware that this very act had stripped them of the last covering that disguised the wrongness of the whole way of living that their violence defended. The law by which he was judged is itself judged, set aside and nailed to the cross. The authorities that publicly shamed him, stripping him naked, have been stripped of their protective covering and exposed as agents of death' - not the agents of life they pretend to be. 'The very Powers that led him to Golgotha are now paraded' as a spectacle for all to see - as they really are! [53]

But the Powers are not the only ones seen for 'who they really are' at Golgotha. Peter courageously confronts the people with their complicity, when he stands up publicly in Jerusalem and says, 'Fellow Jews, and all of you who live in Jerusalem (both Jew and Gentile alike), you know Jesus of Nazareth was a man accredited by God - and *you, you* put him to death!'[54] Jesus may have been put to death by *the powers that be*. But, it was only possible because of the collaboration of *people like you and me*.

Gene Sharp, in his seminal study on *Power and Struggle* says, every Power that there is depends on the support of people for the operationalization of its power. The power that each Power exercises depends on the degree to which people accept its authority, assist with its activities, share their resources with its agencies, and subordinate them selves to its directives. Which people are prepared to do for the Powers out of a sense of obligation, a habit of obedience, the desire for approval, the fear of punishment, the hope of reward, or perhaps just plain laziness - taking the path of least resistance. [55]

Jesus acknowledged that people often 'did not know what they were doing' when they collaborated with the Powers. Even when the crowds, stirred on by the priests, were baying for his blood, he prayed 'Father forgive them, for they know not what they do.'[56]

As Studdert Kennedy, the keen observer and remarkable author of *Indifference* writes, 'All through the ages (people) have crucified God, not knowing what they did. Crucified Him through their ignorance, stupidity, dullness of imagination, feebleness of mind, and a host of other factors - as well as their deliberate choice of wrong against right.'[57]

But at the foot of the cross people are forced to face *the truth* about themselves at last - clearly, unmistakably, and unavoidably. Here, at the foot of the cross, people are forced to confront the truth of *who they are* in the light of *what they have done*. They look at the body in front of them, then look at the blood they have on their hands, and hear that still small voice whispering in their hearts, saying to them: '*You* put him to death, you know.'

There's no time to run. There's no place to hide. They are totally exposed. And stripped of all excuses. They may've been ignorant - but they know ignorance is no justification. They may have been stupid - but they know stupidity is no defense against culpability. They may not have been too bright - occasionally quite dull actually - but they know that lack of imagination is hardly an acceptable explanation for the execution of innocents. As feeble and as fickle as people may have been, they know they must own the truth - that out of some misplaced sense of obligation, habit of obedience, desire for approval, fear of punishment, hope of reward, bout of laziness or fit of spite, they have crucified their Messiah, and they have nobody to blame but themselves!

The Victim Of Injustice At The Heart Of A Hurting World.

Now, according to the scripture, though Christ was crucified, '*once and for all*', as an historical event,[58] Christ is crucified '*afresh*,'[59] in an existential sense, every time *the powers that be,* and *people like you and me,* conspire to crucify one of our neighbours.

Christ makes this very clear when he says '*whatever you do to one of the least*' - one of those that most of you consider the least - the marginalized, distressed, disabled, and disadvantaged - you '*do it to me*'[60]. He says: 'When you help them - you help me. And when you hurt them - you hurt me. Whenever you crucify them - I take it personally - it's as if you are actually crucifying me. "For the wound of the daughter of my people, is my heart wounded - my grief is beyond healing!" '[61]

When we realize Christ is crucified 'afresh,' every time we crucify one of our neighbours, the story of the cross becomes the *metastory* we can use to critically reflect, not only on the role *the powers that be* played in the first century, but also on the role that *people like you and me* play in the twenty-first century.

As Thomas Boomershine, the founder of the Network of Biblical Storytellers, says: 'The story (of the cross) invites us to explore the relationships between our involvement with corporate powers of sin and death (in light of) this narrative of hostility towards Jesus Christ.' A simple way of 'opening ourselves to this tradition' he says, 'is to identify ways in which the groups with which we are identified are involved in sin (and death). To meditate on our involvement in the forces that cause abuse, oppression, poverty, and war.' One way you can do that, he says, is to 'identify a communal situation in which you are involved and listen to the story of Jesus' crucifixion in that context.' [62]

When I look for a 'communal situation' that represents the history of the twentieth century, I can't go past the 'concentration camp'. At the turn of the century the British introduced the concentration camp as a tool for dealing with the Boers. In the middle of the century the Germans developed the concentration camp as an instrument for the 'final solution' of the 'Jewish problem'. And, by the end of the century, the concentration camp was employed in 'killing fields' all over the world - from Cambodia to Kosovo - as the most effective means of pursuing totalitarian policies such as 'cultural revolution and 'ethnic cleansing'. Thus it is that the concentration camp has become the quintessential symbol of cold-blooded brutality in the bloodiest era on earth - signifying the systematic slaughter of hundreds of millions of innocent men, women and children.

The most graphic story I've heard, that connects the concentration camp to the cross, is told by Elie Wiesel in his chilling Nobel prize-winning book <u>Night</u>. Wiesel speaks of an execution he witnessed in Auschwitz when he was a fourteen-year-old boy. Two men and a young boy close to Wiesel's age were suspected of involvement in the sabotage of a power station, and were ordered to be hanged in front of an assembly of prisoners.

> 'One day when we came back from work, we saw three gallows rearing
> up in the assembly place, three black crows. Roll call. S.S. all round us,

machine guns trained: the traditional ceremony. Three victims in chains - and one of them, the little servant, the sad-eyed angel.

The S.S. seemed more preoccupied, more disturbed than usual. To hang a young boy in front of thousands of spectators was no light matter. The head of the camp read the verdict. All eyes were on the child. He was lividly pale, almost calm, biting his lips. The gallows threw its shadow over him.

This time the Lagerkapo refused to act as executioner.

Three SS replaced him.

The three victims mounted together on to the chairs.

The three necks were placed at the same moment within the nooses.

'Long live liberty!' cried the two adults.

But the child was silent.

'Where is God? Where is He?' someone behind me asked.

At a sign from the head of the camp, the three chairs tipped over.

Total silence throughout the camp. On the horizon, the sun was setting.

'Bare your heads!' yelled the head of the camp. His voice was raucous.

We were weeping.

'Cover your head!'

Then the march past began The two adults were no longer alive. Their tongues hung swollen, blue tinged. But the third rope was still moving; being so light, the child was still alive . . .

For more than half an hour he stayed there, struggling between life and death, dying in slow agony under our eyes. And we had to look him full in the face. He was still alive when I passed in front of him. His tongue was still red, his eyes were not yet glazed.

Behind me, I heard the same man asking:

'Where is God now?'

And I heard a voice within me answer him:

'Where is He? Here He is - He is hanging here on this gallows.'[63]

For Elie Wiesel, a deeply religious Jew brought up the Talmud and eager to be initiated into the Cabbala, that evening at sunset became the defining moment of his life.

> 'Never shall I forget that night, the first night in the camp, which has turned my life into one long night, seven times cursed and seven times sealed. Never shall I forget that stroke. Never shall I forget the little faces of the children whose bodies I saw turned into wreaths of smoke beneath a silent blue sky. Never shall I forget those flames which consumed my faith forever. Never shall I forget that nocturnal silence which deprived me, for all eternity, of the desire to live. Never shall I forget those moments which murdered my God and my soul and turned my dreams to dust. Never shall I forget these things…. Never.'[64]

Wiesel never did forget. And neither should we. The powers may want us to forget. The people may want us to forget. We may even want to forget ourselves. But we should never forget - that the way the world is … is literally killing Christ!

In the past few years we have tried to find a way to remind ourselves of this truth in the context in which we live. And we've done it by recycling the Stations of the Cross. The Stations of the Cross are traditional series of meditations on the various stages of the story of the cross, from Jesus' trial through to his crucifixion, his death and his burial. Whereas these meditations used to be more private we have tried to make them more public. Each Easter a group has gone on an open pilgrimage around our city, seeking to identify - and identify with - the places where Christ is still being crucified in our society.

One place we identified that represented where Christ was being crucified today was Brisbane's Planned Parenthood (Abortion) Clinic. 'We may not like to admit it, but we have learned to walk or drive by the(se) specialized killing centres with scarcely a sideways glance or thought as to what goes on behind their doors. We have learned to live with the killing of over 100,000 preborn babies a year (in Australia alone). (And) we have learned to accept (even) partial-birth abortions, where six-month old babies are almost completely delivered alive, only to have to be killed by having their brains sucked out by a vacuum machine. Brisbane's Planned Parenthood (Abortion) Clinic being Australia's specialist centre for this particular technique.'[65]

Another place we identified that represented where Christ was being crucified today was the Tower Mill, on a hill in the middle of Brisbane. The Tower Mill was where the Aborigines who resisted invasion were hanged to death in the early days of settlement. When the first migrants arrived, there were about three hundred thousand Aborigines and Islanders in Australia; but after a hundred years of slaughter and resettlement, there were barely fifty thousand Aborigines and Islanders left alive.[66] Two hundred years later indigenous children still face infant mortality rates three times more than the general population, and a life expectancy of twenty years less than that of any other Australian.[67] And deaths in custody continue to escalate - doubling since the inquiry.[68]

Yet another place we identified that, until recently, represented where Christ was being crucified today was the Recruitment Office for the Australian Armed Forces in Brisbane. Since the invasion and occupation of East Timor in 1975 (until sometime in 1999), the Australian Armed Forces were involved in training of the Indonesian Armed Forces. This included the training of aircraft pilots, combat instructors, military intelligence, and the Special Forces group, Kopassus, who were involved in the wanton massacre of over two hundred thousand people in East Timor. For the Australian Armed Forces to aid the Indonesian Armed Forces in this war against the people of East Timor was particularly reprehensible when you take into account that forty thousand of our nearest neighbours gave their lives to help the diggers fighting the Japanese during the Second World War.

No doubt, former Prime Minister, John Howard, would say this is a 'black-armband' view of history. But, as Justice Marcus Einfeldt says, when it comes to dealing with reality, its much better for us to wear a 'black armband' than it is to wear a 'white blindfold'.

The reason TEAR - a Christian Aid Agency for which I work - exists, is to help Aussie Christians discard their 'white blindfolds' - along with their sets of 'rose coloured glasses' - and discern the presence of the crucified Christ at the heart of our hurting world, which may be getting better for a few, but is getting much worse for the vast majority.

'In the coming world order', says Jacques Attalli, the President of the European Bank for Reconstruction and Development, 'there will be winners and losers. (But) the losers will outnumber the winners by an unimaginable factor. They will yearn for the chance to live decently, and they are likely to be denied that chance.' Then, in a turn of phrase that is reminiscent of the fate of those consigned to the concentration camps, he says, 'they will find themselves penned in, asphyxiated by pollution, neglected by indifference.' And he chillingly concludes: 'the horrors of the twentieth century will fade by comparison.'[69]

Indeed, as we enter the twenty-first century our population is over six billion people, and almost five billion of these live in the 'developing' world. Four-fifths lack basic sanitation. One-third lack clean water. And one-fifth have no access to adequate health services. [70] Sure we give them aid; but they are so indebted, that for every dollar of aid that we give to 'developing' countries, thirteen comes back in interest payments.[71] So after decades of steady advance, aid and development have been thrown into reverse, and over a billion hungry people are sliding, slowly but surely, into the abyss.[72]

'Africa,' Attalli says, 'is a lost continent. It is one of the last places on earth in which famine persists. The terrible facts of having fallen into an economic black hole speak for themselves: since 1970, Africa's share of the worlds markets has been reduced by half; its debt has been multiplied by twenty and now equals its gross product; income in sub-Saharan Africa has fallen by a quarter since 1987. Falling exports and investments, coupled with aging machinery and equipment, guarantees that the economic plight will only grow worse.' And his prediction is dire, saying that 'with the possible exception of South Africa, the most probable future of Africa is tragic: it will be totally... lost.'[73]

Some time back I was asked by TEAR if I would be willing to travel to the Sudan, the largest country in Africa, to assess the current situation there. Needless to say I jumped at the chance to go. But of course I really didn't know what I was getting myself into.

The truth is that the expedition that I made, with Arthur McCutchan, from Kobokor in Northern Uganda to Kajo Keji in Southern Sudan, was one of the most hazardous excursions I have ever done. The road was pocked with bomb craters that were big enough to swallow trucks whole, and roving bands of armed robbers attacked vehicles that broke down on the road. As we were about to leave we heard that a convoy, that had left barely an hour ahead of us, had been shot to pieces by some rebel soldiers.

But we had a job to do, so off we went. The drive to the border went without incident. It was dusk by the time we got to the outpost, and night fell fast and dark. There was no electricity. No light at all. So at the check post we were ordered to stop the car, turn off the headlights, and turn on the inside lights, to illuminate the cabin of the car. We felt like sitting ducks, surrounded by soldiers with their fingers on their triggers, lit up like easy targets in sideshow alley, and not being able to see 'a bloody thing'.

What made us feel even more nervous was the fact that we were traveling on papers issued by the Sudan Peoples Liberation Army, and, at the time we were asked to hand our documents out the window into the darkness, we weren't sure whether the soldiers that had us surrounded were government or guerrilla. The wrong ones - and we could have been in a bit of trouble. Fortunately, it was the SPLA at the border that night.

Across the border we were in Sudan. Sudan has a population of some thirty-five million people. Arab in the arid north. Negroid in the tropical south. They have been at war with one another for twenty-five of the last forty years. It has been a particularly brutal war. Priests have been crucified. Captives sold into slavery. Villages razed to the ground. And vital food stocks destroyed. A million people have died. Five million people have been displaced. And ten million people have been at risk of starving. Government troops stopping emergency food supplies getting to the people in guerrilla held areas.

At first sight its gutted structures gave Kajo Keji the look of a ghost town. But it was inhabited by more than two hundred thousand people. Many of them refugees. Seeking safety away from the fighting. But the bombed out roads and bullet ridden buildings indicated that even here the refugees were caught in the crossfire from time to time.

We met with a local pastor who greeted us warmly and offered to take us to visit some of the camps for displaced people round Kajo Keji. So we spent the day going round the town. Meeting groups of people squatting by the side of the road in temporary shelters made out of sticks and bits of blue plastic. They told us their stories of fleeing on foot, from air raids and ground attacks, across hundreds of kilometres of inhospitable country -side. They all looked as if they'd walked as far as they could, and couldn't walk another step to save themselves. A sign strung across the encampment read: 'Victory Is Assured'. But there was only defeat in the eyes of the bedraggled refugees.

The state of the emaciated people in the camps was serious. But more or less what I had expected. It was the kind of malnutrition that's common in slums all over the world. But then I met the lepers. Outcasts struggling to survive by scavenging on the outskirts of the camps. Without access to a smidgen of the emergency supplies the people in the camps had access to. Not even a single aspirin between them in the last seven years. And nothing that I had ever experienced before - in Afghanistan, Pakistan, India, or Nepal - prepared me for the extremity of suffering I saw reflected in the lepers' eyes. Minus their fingers and their toes, they dragged themselves around the edges of the camps in their skeletally thin bodies. Naked and broken, abandoned and alone, every move they made seemed to scream: *'My God, my God, why have you forsaken me?'*

That night we returned to base in Kajo Keji. I tried to sleep, but couldn't. As I lay there I heard the sounds of screaming. To start with I thought it might have been a domestic dispute. But as the screaming continued a chill crept up my spine as I realized that it probably was some poor man being tortured, or some poor woman being raped. I got up to look around. But I could see nothing at all in the impenetrable darkness. I couldn't see anything. But I heard everything. I heard every howl of torment that was wrung from that wretched soul that night. It was hard for me to lay there listening to the screaming, but it must have been hell for my unseen friend writhing at the hands of those merciless men. At the time the only thing I thought I could do was to pray. So I prayed, desperately, the agony would end. But it went on and on. Like a wound that would never heal. And I asked myself, *'Where is God now?'* And I heard a voice within me answer: *'Where is God now? He is here - writhing in agony at the hands of merciless men!'*

At The Foot Of The Cross - A Confession.

Here we stand at the foot of the cross
Seeing life as it really is.
The frame is hard; the spikes are sharp.
The wounds so raw they weep.

We've always blamed everything on You,
But we're to blame for this blasphemy.
We are Caiphas and Pilate - it's true:
'Better One to die - rather Him than me'.

Some are like Judas, and sell You out.
Some like Peter, leave You high and dry.
Some are like Mary, and want to help,
Only to - helplessly - watch You die.

Some of us sinned for fear;
Some of us sinned for reward;
Some of us sinned for desire;
Some of us sinned for applause.

But, now we know, whenever we sinned,
That, in truth, we sinned against You.

We've crucified You with stupidity.
We've crucified You with spite.
We've crucified You with sophistry.
We've crucified You with style.
We've crucified You with bigotry.
We've crucified You with bias.
We've crucified You with prejudice.
We've crucified You with lies.

We've crucified You with logic.
We've crucified You with law.
We've crucified You with politics.
We've crucified You with power.
We've crucified You with markets.
We've crucified You with trade.

We've crucified You with interest.
We've crucified You with aid.

And now, we don't know what to do,
For, in truth, we have crucified You.

Download lyrics, music and mp3 of "Its Christ That Bleeds" free from:
http://www.daveandrews.com.au/songs/08_christ_that_bleeds.mp3

Ideas For Meditation, Discussion and Action.

1. Why do people blame God for the injustice in the world?

2. What are the implications of projecting the blame onto God?

3. How does the story of the cross absolve God from blame?

4. How are the powers that be implicated by the cross in injustice?

5. How are people like you and me implicated by the cross in injustice?

6. Which of the characters involved in the crucifixion do identify with most? Caiaphas? Pilate? Judas? Peter? Or Mary? How do you feel about that?

7. If you were to take a group of people round your town to show them where Christ was being crucified afresh today in our society, where would you go?

8. What are the powers that be the Jubilee Drop the Debt Campaign identified as having been involved in the crucifixion of Christ in the two-thirds world?

9. When you listen to the radio or watch the news, select one of the stories of suffering that are presented, and try to imagine how Christ feels about it.

10. When you next get your copy of a paper, take it to a quiet place and go over the articles carefully, asking yourself the question: What is my responsibility?

**Some Personal Notes On The Discussions About 'The Cross'
And 'The Tank' at 'Easterfest'.**

On Easter 2010 I went to Easterfest.

Easterfest is Australia's largest Easter festival, which as the promo on the websites says, is 'not just AT Easter, but ABOUT Easter!' Easterfest draws tens of thousands of people from across Australia, who make the pilgrimage up the mountain range to the beautiful regional garden city of Toowoomba.

For four days 'some 200 artists from across the world perform on stages in Queen's Park, as well as cafes, restaurants, pubs, theatres, shopping centres and churches, with music of every kind. From jazz to heavy metal, from acoustic folk to indie pop, from blues, funk and soul to good old rock and roll'.

In and out and around these performances there are presentations by high-profile Christian speakers at the Forum sponsored by the Bible Society. The previous year the Bible Society had asked me to present 'Plan Be' – my take on the Beatitudes as a radical biblical framework for a blessed nonviolent revolution.

This year I had come to Easterfest with no expectation of playing an up-front role. I was there solely to support my wife Ange, and be her back-up, while she was holding her Lastfirst Fair-Trade / Fair-Go stall. However, before this weekend was over, I would unexpectedly find myself very much in the spotlight.

I had helped Ange set up her stall and decided to go for a stroll around the festival to look at what other organisations, such as Compassion, Destiny Rescue and Just Motivation were doing to bring a focus on social justice issues that Easterfest organisers said 'cannot be separated from the message of Easter.'

As I was wandering around I came across a military tent with a tank parked outside. Not a water tank - which are common in our parched part of the world; but a war tank – a heavily-armoured iron-clad fighting vehicle, designed for frontline combat, mounted on all terrain tracks, carrying a large-calibre machine gun.

I was shocked to see a big brutal fire-power fighting vehicle on display at an event which was 'not just AT Easter, but ABOUT Easter!' and talked with the man in uniform who was in charge of the display about it.

'G'day mate'. I said in a friendly voice. 'Could you tell me why you have a tank on display here?'

'The Easterfest organisers invited me to put it on display' the man said, 'as it's an instantly-recognizable eye-catching symbol of ANZAC, and the ANZAC story powerfully illustrates the Easter story of sacrifice'. I was gobsmacked. How could anyone think that the ANZAC story and the Easter story were the same?

But rather than react, I accepted his invitation to watch his documentary on ANZAC. ANZAC stands for Australian and New Zealand Army Corps, whose soldiers were known as Anzacs. When war broke out in 1914 the Anzacs went to war in Europe in support of the British Empire. The documentary told the story.

'In 1915, Australian and New Zealand soldiers formed part of an Allied expedition that set out to capture the Gallipoli Peninsula, according to a plan by Winston Churchill to open the way to the Black Sea for the Allied navies. The ANZAC force landed at Gallipoli on 25 April, meeting fierce resistance from the Ottoman Army commanded by Mustafa Kemal (later known as Atatürk). What had been planned as a bold strike became a stalemate, and the campaign dragged on for eight months.

'At the end of 1915, the Allied forces were evacuated after both sides had suffered heavy casualties and endured great hardships. The Allied casualties included 21,255 from the United Kingdom, an estimated 10,000 dead soldiers from France, 8,709 from Australia and 2,721 from New Zealand. News of the landing at Gallipoli made a profound impact on Australians and New Zealanders at home and 25 April quickly became the day on which they remembered the sacrifice of those who had died in the war. The creation of what became known as an "Anzac legend" became an important part of our national identity.[74]

I had lots of problems with the way the story was told. It glossed over the fact that it was an imperial war that we should have had no part in; that it involved us in an unethical preemptive strike; that it implicated us in the illegal invasion of another country; and that we slaughtered 87,000 Turks at Gallipoli. But in the midst of the slaughter, there were no doubt many examples of heroic self-sacrifice - like Simpson.

So I said to the attendant: 'I'm sure there were many examples of heroic self-sacrifice at ANZAC cove. But if it is sacrifice, not slaughter, that you want to commemorate, wouldn't it better to have a statue of Simpson and his donkey rather than that bloody tank? After all it was Simpson, a stretcher bearer, who commandeered a donkey, wrapped a red cross around its muzzle, and rescued wounded diggers under fire for three and a half weeks until he was killed, who was a real Christ-figure at ANZAC cove.'

'Maybe you're right.' He said. 'But I was asked to bring the tank, so I brought the tank.'

I thanked the attendant and went back to Angie's Lastfirst Fair-Trade / Fair-Go stall to take her a coffee and have a chat about what I should do about the tank. I was deeply disturbed that the organisers had thought that a heavily-armoured iron-clad combat machine, designed to kill people - not to give life, but to take life - was a suitable symbol for Easter, that would somehow communicate the message of Easter.

Overnight I wrote a short flyer about my concerns of having the tank at Easterfest; and the next day gave out my flyers with an invitation for people with similar concerns to meet around the tank early Easter Sunday morning to reflect on the significance of the tank as distinct from the cross as a symbol of Easter.

Most people ignored me. Not many wanted to engage in conversation about the tank. They were too busy enjoying themselves. Which was to be expected. It was a music festival. Not a semiotics seminar. A few people took the flyers. Some said they'd come on Sunday. But most people hurried on to the next gig.

However, even though my actions didn't get much attention, my 'potentially disruptive activities' must have been reported to the management. Because it wasn't long before a couple of broad-shouldered security guards showed up, ordered me to desist and directed me to come with them to the main office.

The manager, Isaac Moody, introduced himself and asked me to sit down. Then, very politely, asked me why I was trying to 'make trouble'. I assured him I wasn't trying to 'make trouble'. If I wanted to 'make trouble', I told him, I could do a much better job. But, he said, you're organizing 'a demonstration'. No, I said, I was only organizing 'a conversation' - about the presence of a tank at Easterfest. But, he said, you're 'causing division'. No, I said, in point of fact you are 'causing division', because you arranged for the tank to be an exhibit at Easterfest, even though the military man warned you it would be contentious.

Okay, Isaac conceded, you may have a point. But, given the fact, it is contentious, and a public debate about the presence of the tank at Easterfest has the potential to ferment a significant level of discontent, if not a completely unprecedented level of disruption, he said, I'd appreciate if you held the conversation off site, rather than holding it on site. I told him that I would be very happy to do that on one condition - that he would agree to meet with me after the festival to discuss the matter face to face. And he agreed.

So we held the public discussion about the tank that Easter Sunday in a local public bar. I asked people what they thought about the significance of the tank, as compared to the cross, as a symbol for Easter.

On the one hand, people thought, it was blasphemous, because they said the tank stood for slaughter, the killing of enemies, whereas the cross stood for sacrifice, a willingness to die to save friend and foe alike. And people thought it was outrageous, that Christians confused the two - and mistook one for the other – as if the inherent violence of the one was the same as the inherent nonviolence of the other.

But on the other hand, people thought, it was ironic, because even though the cross was once a sign of Christ's commitment to nonviolence and sacrifice, since Constantine Christians have taken the cross and used it has a blood-thirsty battle-banner under which they sent in the troops, in recent wars accompanied by tanks, to perpetrate terrible acts of violence and slaughter. And people thought it was tragic, that, as a result of confusing Easter with ANZAC, Christians supported the Allies' invasion of Iraq, even though it was clearly an illegal and unjust war, based on a lie, and had led to the death of over half a million Iraqis.

For some the cross is a sign of ultimate sacrifice. But for others the cross is a sign of imminent slaughter.*

---

* A month or two later I met with Isaac Moody to talk about the tank and the cross. He acknowledged the validity our concerns and said he was open to suggestions as how he might progress further discussions at Easterfest. But in spite of the many suggestions that we made, nothing, as yet, has been forthcoming.

Notes

1   Mark 15:21-37, John 19:30, Luke 23:46
2   Math. 27:39-43
3   Deut. 21:23
4   Mark 15:34
5   John 8:12
6   John 3:19
7   Luke 12:50
8   John 14:31
9   John 10:18
10   John 15:13
11   Josephus *Antiqities* xiii.14.2
12   ibid xvii.10.10
13   Josephus *Wars of the Jews* ii.14.9
14   D.Wiseman 'Crucifixion' *The New Bible Dictionary* Eeerdmans Grand Rapids 1973 p281
15   Math.16:16
16   John 1:1
17   Mark 15:33
18   W.Popkes *Christus Traditus* 1967 p286
19   Ibid p286
20   J.Moltmann ibid p241ff
21   2 Cor. 5:21
22   Acts 8:32
23   D. Soelle ibid pp23-24
24   Heb. 5:8
25   D. Soelle ibid p9
26   H.Ellerbe *The Dark Side Of Christian History* Morningstar San Rafael 1995 ibid p65
27   A, Schmidt *Leviathan* Rowohlt Hamburg 1949 p58
28   Deut.20:16
29   Rom.8:32
30   Math.21:37
31   John 1:11
32   John 3:19-20
33   Math. 20:17-19
34   Math. 26:53
35   Luke 23:46
36   Math.26:56b
37   Math.26:14-16
38   Math.26:69-75
39   Math.27:24-26
40   Math.27:1-2,20-21
41   Math.27:22
42   Luke 23.6-25

43   2 Cor.5:19
44   J.Moltmann *The Way Of Christ* SCM London 1990 p176
45   John 14:9
46   J. Moltmann *The Way Of Christ* SCM London 1990 p173
47   T. McAlpine *Facing The Powers* Marc Monrovia 1991 p15,
48   ibid p12
49   Lesson Outline B.S.H.S. p1
50   Col. 2:15
51   1 Cor. 2:8
52   H.Berkof *Christ and the Powers* Herald Scottdale 1962 pp30ff
53   W.Wink *Engaging The Powers* Fortress Minneapolis 1992 pp139-140
54   Acts 2:22-23
55   G.Sharp *Power and Struggle* Porter Sargent 1973 pp11-12, 18-24
56   Luke 23:34
57   S. Kennedy *The Best Of G.A. Studdert Kennedy* Hodder and Stoughton London
      1963 p84
58   2 Cor.5:15
59   Heb.6:4-6
60   Math.25:40,45
61   Jer.8:21-22
62   T.Boomershine *Story Journey* Abingdon Nashville 1988 p171
63   E.Wiesel *Night* Hill and Wang New York 1960 p 70ff
64   Ibid. Introduction.
65   G.Preston in *Contemporary Christian Issues* Heritage Brisbane 1998 p14
66   D. Andrews *Building A Better World* Albatorss Sutherland p262
67   W.Deane *Some Signposts From Daguragu* Com. Of Australia Canberra 1996 p26
68   P.Dodson *The Path To Reconciliation* Com. Of Australia Canberra 1997 p29
69   J.Attalli *Millennium* Random House New York 1992 p84
70   K.Miller '6 Billion To Feed' *The Courier Mail* Wed. Sept. 22 1999 p19
71   *The Burden of Debt* Jubilee 2000 Coalition 1999 Melbourne p3
72   *The Debt Cutters Handbook* Jubilee 2000 London 1998 p13
73   J. Attalli ibid p73-74
74   http://en.wikipedia.org/wiki/Anzac_Day

"The Cross As Charisma"

Jesus said, 'You know the rulers of the gentiles lord it over them, and their officials expect people to take their orders. (But) the Son of Man did not come to be served, but to serve - and to give his life as a ransom for many. Suppose one of you has a hundred sheep and he lose one of them. Does he not leave the ninety-nine and go in search of the lost sheep until he finds it. And when he finds it, he joyfully puts it on his shoulders and goes home. Then he calls his neighbours and says, "Rejoice with me; I have found my lost sheep." I am the Good Shepherd. I know my sheep, and my sheep know me. I lay down my life for my sheep. Lay it down of my own accord. For I am come that they might have life and have it to the full'.
(Math.20: 25,28; Luke 15:3-6; John 10: 14,11-13,15,10)
That which was from the beginning, which we have heard, which we have seen, and which we have touched - this we proclaim - that Life, that Eternal Life, appeared to us. God so loved the world that He gave His one and only Son that whoever believes in Him should not perish but have Eternal Life. For God didn't send His Son into the world to condemn the world, but that the world, through Him, should be saved. Jesus Christ, the Righteous One, He is the atoning sacrifice for our sins - not only for us, but also for the whole world.
(I John1:1-2; John 3:16-17; I John 2:2)
Day after day every priest stands and performs his religious duties; Again and again he offers the same sacrifices, which can never take away sins. But this Priest offered one sacrifice for all time. We have been made holy through the sacrifice of the body of Jesus Christ, once and for all. So let us draw near to God, in full assurance of faith, having our hearts sprinkled (with the blood of Jesus) to cleanse our guilty consciences.
(Heb.10:11,12,10,22)
If God be for us, who can be against us? He who did not spare his own Son, but gave him up for us all - how will he not also,

along with him, graciously give us all things? God justifies us.
Who can condemn us? Only Christ (whom we killed), and he is
at the right hand of God interceding for us. Who shall separate
us from the love of Christ? Can trouble, pain or persecution?
Lack of clothes or food, danger to life and limb, use of force?
No, in all these things we're more than conquerors through him
who loved us. For I am convinced neither death nor life, angels
nor demons, the present nor the future, the powers above nor
the powers below, nor anything else in God's wide world can
separate us from the love of God in Christ Jesus our Lord.
(Rom.8:31-39)

The Apostle Paul tells us that, when Jesus died on the cross, he died 'for' our sins.[1] However, the critic A. S. Byatt observes 'God sent his "only beloved Son" into the world to die *"for us"*; but the story d(oes) not make it at all clear what *"for"* meant.'[2]

We know that, when Jesus died on the cross, he died 'for' our sins, in the sense that he died 'because of' our sins - because we killed him. Yet Paul insists that he not only died 'because of' our sins, but he also died 'on behalf of' our sin - for 'the sake of' our sins.[3]

The question is - what was it that Jesus did on the cross for 'the sake of' our sins?

This question is not very easy to answer because, as the beloved Scottish theologian, William Barclay, says, 'the church in its wisdom has never had any official doctrine of the atonement. The church has left every(one)' - including critics like A.S. Byatt - 'to find (their) own way to salvation through the life and death of Jesus.'[4]

Nevertheless, this question demands, and deserves, an answer. For, as H.E. Turner says 'no doctrine can represent the fullness of Christian tradition which does not explain *how* the world is made better by the cross.'[5]

To tell you the truth, I don't have *the* answer to this question. But I do have *an* answer - *my* answer. And it is my hope that as you reflect on *my* answer to the question it will help you consider *your* own answer to the question.

The Will Of God.

In order to try to understand what Jesus did on the cross *'for'* our sins, we need to read the story slowly, noting the images that are used to describe the event in the narrative.

John the Baptist introduces Jesus at the beginning of the story as 'the Lamb of God who takes away the sin of the world.'[6] We know the word 'Lamb' is not meant to be taken literally. Jesus was a 'Man' not a 'Lamb'. However, the word 'Lamb' is used to describe the kind of 'Man' that he was. He was a 'Lamb' of a 'Man' - pure and peaceable - as opposed to what many of us would call a 'Wolf in Sheep's Clothing' - duplicitous and dangerous.

According to John the Baptist this 'Lamb' of a 'Man' was also the 'Lamb of God' who would somehow or other 'take away the sin of the world'. John doesn't explain how he expects Jesus to do this; but, in the mind of the people to whom he spoke, there was a very strong association between the figure of a lamb and the ritual of sacrifice, as the people regularly presented a 'lamb without blemish' as an 'offering for their sin'.[7]

Jesus describes the *'sacrifice'* of his life in terms of a *'ransom'* that he is going to pay. He says to his disciples, 'You know the rulers of the gentiles lord it over them, and their officials expect people to take their orders. (But) the Son of Man did not come to be served, but to serve - and to give his life as a *ransom* for many'.[8]

I was brought up to believe the 'ransom' that Jesus paid was a 'literal payment for sin'. As 'only a few find it',[9] only 'a few would be saved' by it. So I thought Jesus must have only paid the price for 'a few' - the 'elect' who were predestined to be saved'

I had big problems with this notion of 'limited atonement'. Not the least was that Jesus contradicted it when he said that he was giving his life *'for many'* (not just *a few*). And his cousin, John the Baptist, seemed to suggest that *'for many'* meant *'anyone'*. After all, Jesus was 'the Lamb of God' who would take away the sin *'of the whole wide world'*.[10]

When I talked to a theologian in my home town about the problems I was having with the notion of the 'limited atonement' in the light of texts that seemed to imply the notion of an 'unlimited atonement', his comments only helped to compound my problems.

He said, 'Dave, what you have to realize is that God doesn't only have one will, he has two - a "revealed will", and a "secret will". His "revealed will" is that "all can be saved" but his "secret will" is that "only some - the elect - will actually be saved".'

To my shame I must confess that for a while I actually took this belief on board as a way of resolving the contradictions inherent in the notion of the 'limited atonement' that I subscribed to at the time. But this belief almost totally destroyed my faith in God.

For if it is true, that God has a "revealed will" and a "secret will", then what God says cannot be taken at face value. And, if it is true, God's "revealed will" is that "all can be saved", but God's "secret will" is that "only some will be saved", then I think, in the final analysis, God can not be trusted.

The mistrust that this belief insinuated into my soul slowly undermined my trust in God.

And I was on the verge of chucking in my faith completely when I decided to revisit the gospels one last time to reevaluate this belief in the light of the bible.

As I read the text again I became convinced that when Jesus said 'Come unto me all you are weary, and I will give you rest', he really meant 'all who are weary' to come.[11] And when one of his disciples said, 'The Lord is not willing that *any* should perish, but that *all* should come to repentance',[12] he meant God's 'secret will' and God's 'revealed will' were really 'one and the same will' - that 'all can be - and all should be - saved'.

With a great sense of relief, I realized that we really could trust God as he comes to us in the person of Jesus Christ. There is no 'secret will' at variance with his 'revealed will'. His 'secret will' is his 'revealed will'. He says what he means, and means what he says.

He says he 'did not come to be served, but to serve - and give his life as a ransom for many' - and he means it - his life is a ransom for 'many' - not just a select, elect 'few'.[13]

Gradually I came to recognize that my problem was not with what Christ had done on the cross, but with my *understanding* of what Christ had done on the cross.

I had interpreted the metaphor of 'ransom' literally, rather than poetically, and consequently interpreted the 'sacrifice' Christ made on the cross as a 'literal payment for sin'. Believing the scripture said in the end 'only a few would be saved', [14] I concluded that Christ must have only 'paid the price' for 'the 'elect', rather than the 'whole wide world'.

A literal interpretation of a poetic metaphor led me to misread what Christ actually did on the cross to such an extent I totally failed to grasp the magnitude of his grace. And I knew that if I was going to grasp the magnitude of his grace again that I would need to handle the old-world metaphors of *'ransom'* and *'sacrifice'* a lot more carefully in future.

Christ As Our Ransom.

Paul says 'There is one God, and one mediator between God and humanity, the man Christ Jesus, who gave himself as a *ransom* for all.'[15] And Peter says that 'you were *ransomed* from the futile ways you inherited from your ancestors, not with silver or gold, but with the precious blood of Christ.'[16]

The word *'ransom'* means 'the price paid for the emancipation or liberation of a person'. In the old world it was the price that was paid to free a slave. While in the modern world it is usually the price that is paid to free a hostage. In both cases the person, for whom a *'ransom'* has been paid, has been 'bought with a price' - a phrase that is repeated like a refrain throughout the epistles.[17]

The image of Christ as *'ransom'* was a powerful metaphor in the first century. Prisoners captured in battle were often taken as slaves and a *'ransom'* was the price that had to be paid in order to secure their freedom. Everyone knew that unless someone paid the price a slave would never be set free. Everything depended on the *'ransom'.*

Unfortunately, during the intervening centuries, people pushed the metaphor too far. To begin with they held the poetic image of the *'ransom'* gently in their hands, and contemplated the implications of the *'ransom'* for themselves as *'slaves to sin'*. It was a dream come true. It meant freedom, from sin, forever! But after a while they took the poetic image of the *'ransom'* and turned it into a soteriological category, which they used to construct a sophisticated theology of salvation. The dream became a nightmare. And freedom from sin got all tied up in philosophical knots.

The big issue was no longer heartfelt appreciation of the One who paid the price, but heady speculation about the one to whom the price was paid. The smart money was on the Devil. Bernard of Clairvaux argued that the Devil is the 'God of this world', people are 'slaves of the Devil and his works', so the 'ransom' must have been paid to the Devil to set us free from sin. He says that because people sinned they are 'justly given over' to the Devil; but because of the price that was paid we are 'mercifully delivered.' And, he adds, there is 'a certain justice in the very deliverance', since, by paying the 'ransom', the Deliverer employed 'justice' in dealing with the Devil, 'rather than power.'[18]

Reformers like Martin Luther came along saying that it was impossible to conceive of the Deliverer dealing with the Devil as an equal. The 'ransom' was not the bargain the Devil thought it was. It was, instead, a rather diabolical trick. Luther says that 'God acts like a fisherman who binds a line to a fishing rod, attaches a sharp hook, fixes a worm, and casts it into the water. The fish comes, sees the worm but not the hook, and bites, thinking he has taken a good morsel, but is caught.' The hook is Christ's divinity. The worm is Christ's humanity. When the Devil tries to snap Christ up, he is caught. 'For Christ sticks in his gills, and, even as he chews Him, the Devil chokes, and is slain.'[19] As Peter the Lombard says, 'the Cross was a trap baited with the blood of Christ.'[20]

I don't know how you feel about this, but I must confess it makes me feel a bit sick. It makes grace seem so grotesque, that I am repelled by it, rather than attracted to it.

Christ As Our Sacrifice.

Offering a 'sacrifice' was a tradition for the Jews that went all the way back to Abraham himself. They had the view that without a 'sacrifice' for sin there could be no salvation.

The Jews said that 'without the shedding of blood there could be no remission of sin.'[21]

Messianic Jews, like Peter, saw 'the precious blood', that was poured out on the cross, as the perfect 'sacrifice' for sin. [22] They poignantly alluded to the ancient prophecy of Isaiah[23] saying: 'All we like sheep have gone astray we have turned every one to their own way, and the Lord has laid on him the iniquity of us all.' They went on to say 'He was wounded for our transgressions, he was bruised for our iniquities: upon him was the chastisement that made us whole - and with his stripes we are healed.'[24]

There is much about this metaphor that we as Gentiles, or non-Jews, find very difficult to understand. But the idea, that someone would be willing to *'sacrifice'* his life for us, is a very powerful story. It touches us with love, in the deep, dark, hidden recesses of our soul, where we feel most unloved, and most unlovable. However, the way this story has often been told, has left many people seeing Jesus as loving - but not God.

According one version of the story, Jesus *'sacrifices'* himself on the altar in order to appease God's anger against sinners who have flagrantly disregarded his holy laws.

Ambrose said, Jesus 'underwent death to give *satisfaction* for those who were under judgment.'[25] Anselm said this *'satisfaction'* was a form of *'compensation'* that had to be paid to God before he could set us free from paying the penalty for our sins ourselves. [26] David Smith sums up this version, when he says, 'we lay, by reason of our sin, under the wrath of God, sentenced to an eternity of torment; and that doom would have been executed upon us, had not Christ offered himself, and suffered in our stead the stroke of God's wrath, and thus appeased his anger and satisfied his justice.'[27]*

For many evangelicals this particular version of events is the correct version. It is 'the gospel'. In my opinion It may indeed be 'good news' for sadists and masochists. But it is not 'good news' for people who desperately need to be able to believe in a loving God.

The problem with presentations of a 'gospel' like this is 'that, in some sense, God and Jesus are opposed. God demands *sacrifice*; Jesus gives *sacrifice*.' William Barclay says presentations such as this 'tend to set Jesus in opposition to God, and they go on to say that something Jesus did in his life - and especially in his death - changed the attitude of God towards (us), and made it possible for God to treat (us) in a different way.'

---

*See Technical Notes at the end of this section for more detail

'When they are stated in their crudest way - when the implication is that God laid on Jesus Christ the punishment which should have been laid upon (us) in order that the divine justice might be maintained - then these interpretations do something even worse. They represent God as protecting his justice by the most monstrous act of injustice the universe has ever seen or ever can see; for he laid on the sinless one the punishment of sin. Even if it be argued that the acceptance by Christ of that situation was completely voluntary and spontaneous, the terrible injustice remains!'

'The result of this is, that almost inevitably Jesus is seen in terms of *love,* and God is seen in terms of *justice'.* Which is 'why a great many people who have been brought up on these interpretations either consciously, or unconsciously, *love* Jesus but *fear* God - (they) feel *at home* with Jesus, but (they) feel *estranged* from God'.[28]

The Cross As Revelation.

To paraphrase the Apostle Paul, let me say, that 'I am convinced neither death nor life, angels nor demons, the present nor the future, the powers above nor the powers below, nor any theology at all, can separate us from the love of God that is in Christ Jesus our Lord.' [29] If our theology of the cross stands in the way of our appreciation of the love of God that is revealed so powerfully on the cross then its time to get rid of our theology.

Many of the interpretations that we have encountered indicate important directions for inquiry. But none of the interpretations, of Christ as 'ransom', or Christ as 'sacrifice', that we have considered, accurately reveal the love of God that was demonstrated in Christ on the cross without some serious distortion. However there is still one more interpret-ation that we might want to ponder. It was put forward by a man named Abelard.

Abelard was born in Brittany in 1079 and died in 1142. He held that Christ did not die, because a ransom had to be paid to the Devil, or because a sacrifice of the blood of an innocent victim was required to appease the anger of God. He held that Christ died as 'a supreme exhibition of love' that 'might kindle a corresponding love in (our) hearts' and 'inspire (us) with the true freedom of (becoming sons and daughters) of God.'

Abelard 'refused to accept any interpretation of Jesus Christ's life and death, which is based on the idea of ransom. Ransom to the Devil is unthinkable.

Ransom to God is unnecessary.' Abelard argued that everything was an expression of the love of God. 'The incarnation of Jesus Christ is an act of pure love. God is righteous, but his right-eousness is his love'.

The problem, as Abelard saw it, 'is that sin has separated (us) from God.' And the solution, as far as Abelard was concerned, 'is to bring (us) back into a relationship of love, and trust, to God. There is no necessity for Christ to assuage the wrath of God, because God's attitude to (us) is not wrath but love. In order to win (us) back to this relationship to God, Jesus Christ has given to (us) the most unanswerable proof of love, a proof of love which so moves (our) hearts that (we) are enabled to enter into the relationship of love with God'. The death of Christ on the cross is not some technical transaction; 'it is rather the supreme evidence of that love which is demonstrated in the life of Christ from the beginning. This love calls forth love, so that we come to "love him because he first loved us".

Abelard went on to say 'that when this love is awakened in our hearts, God forgives us and reckons the merit of Christ to us, in that Christ is the head of the new humanity which begins in him. But the merit of Jesus does not lie in any accumulation of deeds which he did; the merit of Jesus is his obedience to God, and his service of utter love'.[30]

Abelard's interpretation of the death of Christ on the cross emphasizes the fact that it was essentially a revelation of the extent of God's love for us. It was his view: that when God came to us in Christ, and laid down his life for us on the cross, it showed that God loved us so much that there was not anything that he was not willing to do in order to secure our salvation. And this amazing love is the assurance of our hope of salvation.

The Revelation Of Salvation.

There are of course no perfect metaphors, no perfect interpretations, and no perfect explanations for what it was that Christ did for us on the cross. Each of the metaphors and each of the interpretations are finite attempts to plumb the depths of an indefinable event that defies full explanation. So, while we should be suspicious of explanations that claim to be *true truth*, we should learn as much as we can from these explanations, in order to seek to understand *more truly* what it was that Christ did on the cross for us.

I feel we have much to learn, and much to re-learn, from the Abelard's interpretation of the death of Christ as a *revelation* of the extent of God's love for us. But we don't have to throw out the metaphors of *ransom* and *sacrifice* - like Abelard did - in the process.

The scriptures are quite clear on this point. Christ is our *ransom*. Christ is our *sacrifice*. So instead of rejecting the metaphors, we would be better off if we were to reframe our interpretation of *ransom* and *sacrifice* in the light of the *revelation* of God's love for us.

The metaphor of Christ as our *ransom* was a powerful metaphor in the first century. Prisoners captured in battle were often taken as slaves and their *ransom* was the price that had to be paid in order to secure their freedom. They knew that unless someone paid the price for their salvation they would never be free. So they prayed for someone who would be willing to pay their *ransom* more than they prayed for anything else.

During the Battle of Adrianople, in the fourth century, many prisoners were captured. A message about their plight, with a plea for help, was sent to Ambrose, the Bishop of Milan. Ambrose lived simply, having already given away most of his possessions to help the poor, but he was determined to raise the money needed for a *ransom* to secure their release. So he took the sacred vessels of the sacrament from off the altar of his church, melted them down, and turned the gold and silver containers into gold and silver coins. He then went and spent all the money he'd collected to ransom the captives. Inevitably there were parishioners who accused Ambrose of acting sacrilegiously. But the Bishop answered his accusers, by saying that the people - for whom Christ's body was broken and Christ's blood was shed - were much more precious than the vessels that carried the symbols of his sacrificial love for them.[31]

Now, whenever I tell this story, no one ever says to me - 'tell me, Dave, who was it that they paid the *ransom* to?' No one is interested in that. Because that's beside the point.

Instead, everyone says to me, 'tell us, again, who was that guy who paid the *ransom*?' Every one is interested in that. Because that's what the whole point of the *ransom* story is. The *ransom* story is all about *someone who is prepared to give everything he's got to save someone else.* Which is why the *ransom* story is such a beautiful picture of what God did for us in Christ.

The metaphor of Christ as someone who was willing to *sacrifice* himself on our behalf can be as powerful a metaphor in the twenty-first century as it was in the first century.

There is much about the way the Jews might understand this metaphor that we, as non-Jews, find very difficult to understand. But the idea, that someone would be willing to *'sacrifice'* his life for us, is a very powerful story. That touches us with love, in the deep, dark, hidden recesses of our soul, where we feel most abandoned, and most alone.

Telemachus was a monk in the fourth century that lived more or less contentedly in a remote Asiatic Christian community. Then one day, Telemachus sensed that the Spirit was encouraging him to leave his community and go to Rome, which at that time, was like the capital of the world. When Telemachus arrived in the so-called 'heavenly city', Rome was celebrating a recent victory of its powerful legions over the troublesome Goths, and so, for the holiday festival, a circus was being staged for the jubilant multitudes.

Telemachus didn't know where he was going. But he allowed himself to be swept along by the crowds on their way to the Coliseum for the circus. When the crowds arrived at the Coliseum they began to get excited at the sound of the lions roaring their challenge and the gladiators preparing for combat. Telemachus didn't know what he was doing. But he followed the crowd into the Coliseum, where, to his horror, he was confronted with gut-wrenching carnage, as gladiators fought one another to the death, slaughtering their hapless foes, without pity, as a red-blooded entertainment for the blood-thirsty crowds.

It was all too much for Telemachus. He felt that he had to do something. He simply couldn't stand by idly and do nothing while human beings were being beheaded, disemboweled, and dismembered before his very eyes. So Telemachus ran down the steps of the stands, leapt into the arena, and began darting, back and forth between the fighters, crying, 'Forbear. Forbear. In the name of Christ I beg you to forbear.'

When the crowd saw the scrawny figure of the monk, running frantically about the arena, ducking and weaving between the combatants, to start with, they took Telemach-us to be a bit of welcome comic relief, and roared their approval. But as time went by, some of the people in the crowd began to hear what 'the mad monk' was saying, and, as more and more of the crowd came to realize that Telemachus was actually trying to spoil their bloody fun, they turned against him, hissing, and booing, and bellowing at the top of their voices for his quick dispatch.

What happened next no one seems to know for sure. We do know that the gladiators lunged at the monk with thrusts from their swords; and we do know that the audience buried the monk under a hailstorm of stones. But we do not know for sure whether it was the gladiators, or the audience, that killed him. All that we know is that, when the furor was over, Telemachus lay dead in the middle of the arena.

Then a strange thing happened. In the silence that ensued, it was if the monk's last cry echoed eerily around the arena once again: 'Forbear. Forbear. In the name of Christ I beg you to forbear.' Overcome with shame, the spectators departed, leaving the circus empty, never to return. Never again did an audience gather to watch people butcher each other at the Coliseum in Rome. All brutal gladiatorial battles were banned. And Telemachus was written into the pages of history as the hero who, single-handedly, brought the era of slaughter as entertainment to an end.

Probably, the declining power of the empire, resulting in diminishing numbers of recruits for gladiatorial schools, and decreasing amounts of funds available to stage gladiatorial contests, were also very significant factors in putting an end to the circus; but Telemachus will always be remembered as the man who, in the end, was actually prepared to *sacrifice* his life to save people in the arena from slaughter.[32]

When I talk to people about this story, the issue of 'who the *sacrifice* was made to' never comes up. Because it is not the issue. An issue that does come up is 'who the *sacrifice* made was for.' Because that is obviously an issue of importance in the story. The story is about saving people in the arena from slaughter. However, the issue that comes up for discussion most of the time is 'who the guy was who made the *sacrifice*.' Because the *sacrifice* story is all about *someone who is prepared to lay down their own life to save the lives of others*. Which is why *sacrifice* is such a magnificent picture of what God did for us in Christ.

Thus, if we reframe our interpretation of the metaphors of *ransom* and *sacrifice* in the light of the *revelation* of God's love, what God did for us on the cross in Christ is clear. On the cross God proved to us, once and for all, beyond any shadow of a doubt, that he is the kind of person who is always prepared to give everything he's got to help some- one else, even to the extent of laying down his own life, to save the lives of others.

This is the gospel. This is the good news. That God is indeed good. So good, in fact, that he is far better than we could have ever imagined that he might be. He is actually willing to give everything he's got in order to help us - even to the extent of being willing to lay down his own life for us. Jesus' life and death is God's guarantee of our salvation.

But the question remains - why the necessity of this *sacrifice* for the forgiveness of sins? - why the necessity of having to pay such a heavy price, in blood, to *ransom* our souls?

There is no biblical evidence to suggest that the *ransom* was the price paid to the Devil. And there is no biblical evidence to suggest that the *sacrifice* was offered to God to give him his 'pound of flesh' before he was willing to forgive us. Quite to the contrary. The scripture says God is always more than willing to forgive and being willing to forgive means being willing to relinquish any right to retaliation - the opposite of demanding any kind of vindictive satisfaction. So to say that God required some kind of bloody vindictive satisfaction before he could forgive us is not only totally untrue - but also utterly absurd.

So why, we may ask, the need for Christ to be 'the atoning sacrifice for our sins?' [33]

My view is that there never was, and never will be, any forgiveness without *sacrifice*. Forgiveness, by definition, means making the sacrifice that is necessary to accept an injustice without demanding satisfaction in return. The greatness of any single act of forgiveness consists in the greatness of the *sacrifice* that a person is prepared to make in relinquishing their right to restitution or retaliation in order to restore a relationship. The greatness of forgiveness is in exact proportion to the greatness of the *sacrifice*.

It is my view that throughout the ages God had always been prepared to suffer greatly to forgive greatly. But because God was invisible, no one saw the tears that God cried.

Only the prophets, who lived in sympathy with the heart of God, had any appreciation of the greatness of his *grace*. Until, at the right time, God stepped onto the stage of human history, visibly, as a human being, and, in Jesus, shows us just how great his *grace* is.

God's *grace* is great enough to *embrace our pain, absorb our rage, forgive our sin*, and *encourage us all towards completely revolutionary personal growth and social change.*

In Jesus on the cross, we can see that God embraces our pain. Frederick Beuchner tells a story that he says is 'a peculiarly twentieth century story'. And you only have to hear the story once to know it's just the kind of story that Jesus himself might have told. 'It's a kind of parable of the lives of all of us. It's about a boy of twelve or thirteen who, in a fit of crazy anger got hold of a gun and fired it at his father, who did not die straight away but soon afterward. When (he) was asked why he had done it, he said that he could not stand his father, because his father demanded too much of him. And then later on, after he had been placed in a house of detention, a guard was walking down the corridor late one night when he heard sounds from the boy's room, and he stopped to listen. The words that he heard the boy sobbing out in the dark were, "I want my father, I want my father". 'Our father', Beuchner says, 'we have killed him, and we will kill him again.'[34] But Jesus, on the cross cries out, as one of us, saying "Father. Forgive them. For (I know) they know not what they do".

In Jesus on the cross, we see God not only embraces our pain, he also absorbs our rage. As Gale Webbe, in *The Night and Nothing,* said, 'There are many ways to deal with evil. All of them are facets of the truth that the only ultimate way to conquer evil is to let it be smothered within a willing, living, human being. When it is absorbed there, like a spear into one's heart, it loses its power and goes no further.'[35] As Scott Peck says in The People Of The Lie , 'The healing of evil can only be accomplished by love. A willing sacrifice is required. The healer must sacrificially absorb the evil.'[36] Jesus on the cross absorbed our evil. He took into his heart as assuredly as the spear that was thrust into his side. And, it went no further. There was no reaction.

No demand for restitution. No demand for retaliation. The cycle of violence stopped right there and then, with him, forever.

In Jesus on the cross, we see God not only absorbs our rage, he also forgives our sin. 'One thing I know', William Barclay says, 'that because of Jesus Christ and what he did (on the cross) my relationship to God is changed. Prior to Jesus Christ (we) did not fully know what God was like. The holiness of God (we) did know; but the marvel of the love of God (we) had never dreamed of. When Jesus healed the sick, comforted the sad, fed the hungry and forgave his enemies, he was saying, "God loves you like that. Nothing that (you) can ever do will stop God loving (you)." Because of Jesus Christ I know God is my friend. He is no longer my enemy. He is no longer even my judge. There is no longer any unbridgeable gulf between him and me. Daily, and hourly, I experience the fact that I can enter into his presence with confidence. (And as a result) I am more at home with God than I am with any other human being in the human world'.[37]

Last, but not least, in Jesus on the cross we see God not only forgives our sin, he also encourages us all towards completely revolutionary personal growth and social change. When I gaze at Jesus on the cross my heart is strangely moved. Someone dying for a cause doesn't make it right. But a manifesto of love written in blood can not be easily dismissed. A movement, which has proved to be worth dying for, may lay claim to be worth living for. The martyrdom of Jesus lights a beacon for compassion - an inexting-uishable fire that scorches the apathy and hypocrisy hidden in the dark corners of my soul. His agony breaks my heart, and, in the process, breaks down some of my barriers I have erected in my heart against my own humanity. His anguish brings the sound of others crying to my ears which otherwise I would not hear, and brings the sight of others suffering to my eyes which otherwise I would not see. For me, the death of Jesus is not the end, but the beginning - of a whole new way of life committed to the way of Jesus.

Grace For The Struggle.

TEAR Australia is an agency that exists to help Aussie Christians struggle with injustice in the world in the light of the amazing grace that God revealed to us in Jesus Christ. Through TEAR publications and presentations Aussie Christians are reminded that we do not struggle with oppression and poverty and starvation and war in a vacuum - we are called to struggle with life and death issues in the context of the life and death of Jesus.

Steve Bradbury, the former director of TEAR, says quite unashamedly, 'We do indeed have good news to share' with the people who are concerned about saving the planet.

'Because Jesus came', he says, 'we can know with certainty that the creation, and all who are in it, are profoundly loved by the Creator.' The 'God of grace' revealed 'in Jesus' is with us in our struggle against injustice. 'What is more', he says, 'there is great joy in knowing that there will come a time when Jesus will finish what he has begun', and 'the sadness' that we struggle with - day after day - one day 'will be no more.'[38]

This is a theme Steve goes back to time and again in his editorials for *Target* magazine. In a column entitled '*That Gentle Heart*', Steve writes: 'During our summer holiday my wife discovered, in the bookshelves of friends we were staying with, an old book that I had wanted to read for years. "*The Christ Of The Indian Road*" written by E. Stanley Jones, and published in 1926, is a missionary classic. It really is worth a careful read.

Consider this: "if God thinks in terms of little children as Jesus did, cares for the leper and the outcast, and, if his heart is like that gentle heart, that broke upon the cross, then he can have my heart without reservation". Jones is describing the God I know (in) Jesus. Were God not like this', Steve says, 'I would not want to be found among his worshippers.' Then, Steve goes on to say, what I have heard others say in TEAR circles round Australia, 'I want to know Jesus better....The One who was nailed to the cross for the sins of the world, loves the poor and hates the systems which continue to crucify them....I want to follow him more closely, and reflect his love more completely'. [39]

In Brisbane over the last few years we've started a number of TEAR support groups that meet regularly to help people draw on the grace of 'that gentle heart that broke upon the cross' - that Steve alluded to - to sustain us in our struggle against injustice. Once every four weeks I meet with the Tim Tam group at Brookfield, the Fruit Cake group at Aspley, and the Fatfree Muffin group at West End. We usually start our meetings with a cuppa and a serving of the specialty of the house. Tim Tams at Richard and Trish's, Fruit

Cake at Frank and Val's, and Fatfree Muffins at Lindsay and Katherine's. Then, from 7.30 to 9.00 pm, we get down to some serious work, spending the next one and a half hours re-reading the scriptures, re-membering the story, and re-working our responses to issues in the light of the gospel.

At the heart of the process is a story telling segment where someone tells a story of an issue they are struggling with. As this is confidential, I can't tell who told what story, but I can tell you some of the issues that we are struggling with. As Australians all of us are struggling with the original sin of Australia - the dispossession of Aboriginal and Islander peoples. We are painfully aware of our country's unwillingness, as yet, to repent of our sin, seek true reconciliation and make real restitution for a crime from which we benefit. Some of us have examined our investments and discovered, to our shame, that some of our superannuation funds have been invested in companies that are manufacturing armaments and destroying the environment. While others, who have gone overseas to work with the poor, are living with the guilt of having returned home safely, to live in relative luxury, while the friends whom we made while overseas struggle to survive.

As we share these stories it is not uncommon for us to feel overwhelmed by the pain. Without due care our shame can become rage and our guilt can become despair. We can easily become totally debilitated by our unmediated reactions to these issues. But we make sure that we never finish sharing about our stories without praying about our stories. It is in prayer we are able to deal with our feelings with the care they require. We may be tempted to feel totally debilitated, however, through prayer we can process our responses, and make them much more pro-active than re-active. For it is in the light of grace we find that we are able to consider our responses more constructively and productively. Grace helps us acknowledge our faults, accept our limitations and contra-dictions, develop discernment in the midst of confusion, energy when we would have otherwise exhausted our resources and endurance where we would have otherwise run out of patience. It is only through grace we feel we can enter into the struggle for justice.

Through grace we have managed to stumble slowly, but surely, step by step, towards doing more and more justice to the issues that our groups are concerned about.

Most of us have been involved in the movement of Australians For Reconciliation in one way or another. Arthur managed to get to the Australian Reconciliation Convention. A few of us have joined ANTaR, Australians for Native Title and Reconciliation. Peter has helped set up a local group called 'Pay The Rent', which not only recognizes prior ownership of the land, but also provides a way for us to pay rent to the traditional owners of the land on which we now live. A number of us also continue to support the ministry of Aunty Jean, a well-known, long-serving Aboriginal leader in our community. While Steve and Emma, a doctor and a lawyer respectively, have chosen to move to Katherine, in the Northern Territory, in order to help provide good quality medical and legal services to local Aboriginal communities in the Territory.

Many of us have reviewed our investments. Helen transferred her investment money into an ethical investment fund, challenging the rest of us to do the same. Some of us signed up with Australian Ethical Investment, which is committed to investments that contribute to a just and sustainable world.

All of us continue to reassess our commitment to the poor each time that we meet. Most of us give to the poor through TEAR. Many of us are partners, giving regularly to TEAR by direct debits from our bank accounts. Ralph and Susan decided to go to Melbourne so Ralph could work with TEAR, and now works for Servants To Asia's Urban Poor. Just about everybody has been involved in the Jubilee Drop The Debt Campaign, advocating the cancellation of the unpayable debt of the world's most highly indebted poor countries. Frank and Val, Allan and Nadine, David and Ruth, Greg and Katie, Brett and Annette, Richard and Trish, Helen, Arthur, and Sannie all 'did the hard yards'. Meanwhile Mark and Kathy, and Greg and Katie actually returned to work in India. And Brett and Annette also decided to work in Delhi for a while. Mark and Kathy work in the slums with Servants To Asia's Urban Poor. Greg and Katie worked for marginalised and disadvantaged people with Sharan. And Brett and Annette worked for distraught and distressed people with Sahara. Until their retirement, Frank and Val regularly returned to the subcontinent to do locums in hospitals and run support groups for doctors in the Emmanuel Hospital Association. While David has continued to do really significant ground-breaking work with Bible Societies throughout the whole of Asia.

The Face Of Compassion - A Celebration.

Strung out - naked - on the cross;
    Your body battered by our rage.
We see the cuts; we hear the cries;
    But search in vain for our disgrace.

Around your brows form lines of kindness.
    In your eyes - a look of care.
Down your cheeks flow tears of sadness.
    On your lips - a word of prayer.

    What grace is this?
    As strong as death!
    Taking the bad, along with the good.

    What peace is this?
    As soft as breath!
    Understanding, tho' misunderstood.

As we sense your love embrace us,
    We all feel a great relief.
Here - at last - is our forgiveness!
    Now - at last - we can be free!

    What bliss is this?
    As bright as light!
    Banishing shadows day and night.

    What glow is this?
    As warm as fire!
    Infusing our lives with true desire.

We no longer need be fearful,
    Of the many times we've failed.
We can start to be more hopeful.
    In your presence love prevails.

Love never looked so sorrowful.
    Love never looked so sore.
Love never looked so beautiful.
    Love never looked so pure.

Love never looked so tangible.
Love never looked so great.
Love never looked so lovable.
As it looks - upon your face.

Download lyrics, music and mp3 of "What Love Is This?" free from:
http://www.daveandrews.com.au/songs/09_what_love_is_this.mp3

Ideas For Meditation, Discussion and Action.

1. Why do you think that people doubt God's desire to save the world?

2. What are the implications of doubting God's desire to save the world?

3. How does the story of the cross demonstrate God love for the world?

4. How would you explain your own view of Christ as our 'salvation'?

5. Barclay says 'Because of Christ I know God is my friend. He is no longer my enemy. He is no longer even my judge. There is no longer any gulf between him and me. Daily I experience the fact that I can enter into his presence with confidence'. What is your experience of Christ yourself?

6. What is the role of a support group in the struggle for justice?

7. What is the significance of being able to tell one another our story?

8. What is an issue of injustice in the world that you are struggling with?

9. How is your own experience of grace related to your struggle for justice?

10. Through grace we have managed to stumble slowly, step by step, towards doing justice to the issues our groups are concerned about. What is the next step that you believe you ought to take in order to be more faithful to Christ's call upon your life to really care for the poor?

Some Technical Notes On The Notions Of 'Propitiation' And 'Expiation' and Salvation.

Now I know many Christians agree with David Smith, when he says, 'we lay, by reason of our sin, under the wrath of God, sentenced to an eternity of torment; and that doom would have been executed upon us, had not Christ offered himself, and suffered in our stead the stroke of God's wrath, and thus appeased his anger and satisfied his justice.'[40] And when I say to them that I disagree with David Smith, they jump to the conclusion that I don't believe 'we lay, by reason of our sin, under the wrath of God'; and/or that I don't believe that we were doomed, 'had not Christ offered himself, and suffered for us, on our behalf.

So, let me say it, loud and clear - I do believe that 'we lay, by reason of our sin, under the wrath of God', and I do believe that we were doomed, 'had not Christ offered himself, and suffered for us, on our behalf.

However, let me say it, equally loudly and equally clearly - I do *not* believe that God scapegoated Christ. Christ bore *our* wrath - *not* God's - when we put him to death on the cross. And, in dying, and in rising again, without any sign of the slightest desire for retaliation, retribution or revenge, he ensured us of his forgiveness, that is so great, that it guarantees the salvation of all who would 'be-lieve' it and 'live-by' it.

The Apostle John writes, 'We have an advocate with the Father, Jesus Christ the righteous, and he is the *propitiation* for our sins' (1 John 2:1-2); and 'Here is love, not that we loved God, but that he loved us, and sent his Son to be a *propitiation* for our sins' (1 John 4:10). And, the Apostle Paul writes, 'Christ Jesus ...God sent forth to be a *propitiation* through faith in his blood.' (Romans. 3:24-25)

In these passages, the Greek word, *'hilasmos'*, is often translated into English as *'propitiation'*, which means *'to appease - or pacify - anger.'* [41] So, according to these translations, it might seem that Smith's notion, that 'Christ suffered to appease - or pacify - the anger of God', might be correct after all.

However, history teaches us, over and over again, that things are not always the way they seem to be.

The New Testament scholar, C.H. Dodd translates 'hilasmos', as 'expiation', not 'propitiation'. He says 'most translators (who translate 'hilasmos' as 'propitiation') are wrong.' He says, 'the meaning conveyed ... is that of expiation, not that of propitiation.' [42] Whereas propitiation would indicate 'assuaging God's anger', expiation, would indicate 'assuaging our own guilt'. And Dodd asserts that 'Hellenistic Judaism, as represented by the LXX, does not regard the cultus as a means of pacifying the displeasure of the Deity (propitiation), but as delivering man from sin (expiation).' [43] 'The performance of prescribed rituals ... had the value, so to speak, of a powerful disinfectant' cleansing the soul from sin. [44]

Many evangelicals would dismiss Dodd's views as liberal, but the well-known, and well-regarded evangelical scholar, John Stott, agrees with Dodd, that 'Jesus, as the *hilasmos* in relation to our sins, (1 John 2:2; 1 John 4:10) *could be understood as meaning simply that he took them away, or cancelled them.'* [45] (italics mine)

However, 'as for the passage in Romans 3', Stott says, 'the context is determinative'. He says, 'Jesus is set forth by God as a universal remedy for human guilt under his wrath.' [46]

Now, I am not in a position to know whether Stott is right in this regard, or not. But, for arguments sake, let us assume that he is, and that, in Romans, at least, 'Jesus is set forth by God as a universal remedy for human guilt under his wrath.'

If we go back to the actual passage in Romans that Stott is quoting from, it is important to note that Paul writes that 'Christ Jesus' was 'sent forth to be a propitiation' - not 'through his blood' - but 'through faith in his blood.' (Rom. 3:24-25) The wrath of God is not pacified by the blood of Christ but by 'faith in his blood'.

Which means God's anger about the sin in our lives is not appeased by Christ's sacrifice on the cross, but by our response to that sacrifice - by our sanctification - our transformation - 'through faith in his blood'.

Notes

1	1 Cor.!5:3
2	A. S. Byatt ibid p73
3	1 Cor.15:3
4	W Barclay ibid p95
5	H.E. Turner ibid p46
6	John 1:29
7	Lev.4:32-35
8	Math.20:25,28
9	Math.7:13
10	John 1:29
11	Math.11:28
12	2 Pet.3:9
13	Math.20:25,28
14	Math.7:13
15	1 Tim.2:5
16	1 Pet.1:18
17	1 Cor.6:20;7:23; Gal.3:13;4:4
18	W. Barclay ibid p119
19	G.Aulen *Christus Victor* McMillan New York 1969 pp103-104
20	W.Barclay ibid p121
21	Heb.9:22
22	1 Pet.1:18
23	I Pet.2:24-25
24	Isa.53:5-6
25	W.Barclay ibid p118
26	G.Aulen ibid p93
27	W.Barclay ibid p116
28	W.Barclay ibid pp122-124
29	Rom.8:38-39

30   W.Barclay ibid pp124-125
31   W.Barclay ibid p109
32   D.Andrews The Mad Monk *Target* Summer 2000 p19
33   1 John 1:1-2; John 3:16-17; 1 John 2:2
34   F. Beuchner *The Magnificent Defeat* Harper Collins San Francisco 1966 p65
35   G.Webbe *The Night and Nothing* Seabury Press New York 1964 p109
36   S. Peck *The People Of The Lie* Simon & Schuster New York 1983 p269
37   W. Barclay ibid p134,130,129
38   S.Bradbury 'Do Justice, Love Kindess, Walk Humbly With God', *Target* No.3 1998 p17
39   S.Bradbury 'That Gentle Heart' *Target* No.3 1998 p1 (edited)
40   W.Barclay ibid p116
41   J.Stott *The Cross Of Christ* IVP 1986 p169
42   C.H.Dodd *The Bible And The Greeks* 1935 Hodder and Stoughton p94
43   ibid p93
44   C.H Dodd *Johannine Epistles* Hodder And Stoughton 1946 p25-26
45   J.Stott *The Cross Of Christ* IVP 1986 p172
46   ibid p172

"The Cross As Catalyst".

*The Lord Jesus, on the night he was betrayed, took bread, and
When he had given thanks, he broke it and said, 'This is my body
given for you; do this in remembrance of me.' In the same way,
after supper he took the cup, saying, 'This the new covenant in
my blood poured out for you; do this, whenever you drink it, in
remembrance of me.'* (1 Cor.11:23-25)

*Then Jesus said to them, 'A new commandment I give to you:
that you love one another as I have loved you. People can have
no greater love than this - than to give their life for their friends.
If anyone would come after me, let them deny themselves, take
up their cross, daily, and follow me. Whoever wants to save their
life will lose it, but whoever loses their life, for me, will save it.'*
(Luke 9:23-24; John 15:12-13)

*If we confess our sins, he will forgive our sins, and the blood
of Jesus will cleanse us from all unrighteousness (injustice).
If we keep on sinning after we have received the knowledge
of the truth, no sacrifice for sins is left, only judgment. How
severely do you think someone deserves to be punished who
has trampled the Son of God under foot, and treated like dirt
the blood of the covenant that had once made them holy?*
(1 John 1:7,9; Heb.10:26-29)

*Christ suffered for you, leaving you a personal example, so
that you should follow in his footsteps. Your attitude should
be the very same as that of Christ: who did not cling to his
prerogatives as God, but emptied himself of all privileges, in
becoming a human being, indeed a servant of human beings,
and being obedient even unto death, even death on a cross.*
(1 Pet.2:21; Phil.2:5-8)

*God is love. Whoever lives in love lives in God, and God
lives in them. Whoever loves, knows God. Whoever does
not love, does not know God. For God is love. This is love:
not that we loved God, but that he loved us. This is how we*

know what love is: Jesus Christ laid down his life for us. And
we ought to lay down our lives for one another. If anyone is
well-to-do and sees someone in want and shuts their eyes -
and their heart - how can anyone believe the love of God lives
in them? Let us love, not merely in theory, as policy, but in
sincerity and in reality - in truth.

(1 John 4:16,7-10;3:16-18)

One of the problems people have with Christians is that we are not only un-Christ-like, but we also use our Christian theology to rationalize our continuing to be un-Christ-like. After all - as the bumper stickers emblazoned on our Volvos boldly proclaim - we're: 'Not perfect - Just forgiven!'

This sticks in the throats of many non-Christians who hoped Christians might be better. And they grumble about us as we drive by; especially as we drive by - without picking them up - when they are hitching on the side of the road; and we leave them - standing in the pouring rain - unaided.

Justification As Rationalization?

Mahatma Gandhi was a non-Christian who was not afraid to confront Christians with our misuse of the theology of the cross in rationalizing our continued un-Christ-likeness.

In his famous story about his *Experiments With Truth*, Gandhi describes an encounter he had with an evangelical Christian. 'Mr Coates was a staunch young man', he says. And 'he introduced me to several friends whom he regarded as staunch Christians. One of these introductions was to a family that belonged to the Plymouth Brethren.'

'During my contact with this family', Gandhi says, 'the Plymouth Brethren confronted me with an argument for which I was not prepared:

"You cannot understand the beauty of our religion. You must be brooding over your transgressions every moment of your life, always mending themand atoning for them. How can this ceaseless cycle of action bring you re-demption? You can never have peace.

Now look at the perfection of our belief. You admit we are all sinners. Our attempts at improvement are futile. Yet redemption we must have. How can we bear the burden of sin? We can but throw it on Jesus. He is the only sin-less Son of God. It is his word that those who believe in him

72

shall have ever-lasting life. As we believe in the atonement of Jesus, our own sins do not bindus. Sin we must. It is impossible to live in this world sinless. Therefore Jesusatoned for all the sins of (hu)mankind. Only he who accepts his great redemption can have eternal peace.

Think what a life of restlessness is yours - what a promise of peace we have".

Many Christians would have thought this was a pretty convincing presentation of the gospel, but the non-Christian Gandhi says that 'the argument failed to convince me.'

And the reason that this presentation of the gospel failed to convince Gandhiji is worth considering. Gandhi says, 'I humbly replied:

"If this be Christianity acknowledged by all Christians, I cannot accept it. (For) I do not seek redemption from the consequences of my sin. I seek to be redeemed from sin itself - (even) the very thought of sin. Until I have attained that, I shall be content to be restless".'[1]

Gandhi did not question the theology of the cross that he was presented with because he wanted to 'continue in unrighteousness'. Quite the contrary. Gandhi said that he desired to be righteous with all his heart - 'to be redeemed from sin ' - not merely 'the consequences of sin'. He questioned the theology of the cross he was presented with because he felt that it was being used as a rationalization for continuing in sin. 'Sin we must.' It went. 'It is impossible to live in this world sinless'. Only Jesus 'is sinless'.

Now I think that it is quite interesting to note that a number of the Apostles had similar concerns about this process of theological rationalization as the Mahatma himself had.

Paul asked the question: 'Shall we sin because we are not under law but under grace?' And his own resolute answer to the question comes down to us through the centuries, as clearly as ever, crying - 'Never! Your body should be an instrument of righteousness.' [2]

John writes, 'If we confess our sins, he will forgive our sins, and the blood of Jesus will cleanse us' - not only from the consequences of unrighteousness, but also from, what he calls, 'all unrighteousness', itself. [3]

In the letter written to the *Hebrews* this issue - of cleansing 'from all unrighteousness' - is discussed in detail. It is clear that Messianic Jews were aware of the limitations of their traditional 'sacrifices' to effect real change. 'The blood of goats sprinkled on those who are ceremonially unclean', they said, only 'makes them outwardly (not inwardly) clean.'[4] But, they said, when the 'Lamb of God' came along, and gave himself as a 'sacrifice' on their behalf, they thought this would change everything for them forever - inside and out. 'How much more' (than the blood of goats) 'will the blood of Christ cleanse our consciences from acts that lead to death - to serve the living God!'[5]

They went on to say, quite categorically, 'if we keep on sinning after we have received the knowledge of the truth, no sacrifice for sins is left, only judgment. How severely do you think someone deserves to be punished who has trampled the Son of God under foot, and treated like dirt the blood of the covenant that had once made them holy?'[6]

Now this is not a view that is espoused in most of the Christian circles in which I move. It is considered to be 'too heavy', 'too harsh', 'too judgmental' and 'too ungracious' to be Christian. But, believe it or not, it is exactly the same view that Christ himself expressed.

No Salvation Without Grace.

Many Christians believe that, because salvation is unmerited, it is also unconditional. They argue that, because we cannot say or do anything to earn our salvation, then nothing that we can say or do can put our salvation in jeopardy. Which, I must admit is quite a comforting thing to believe. I'd like to believe it myself. But, unfortunately, like many comforting beliefs, it is completely false. In the corpus of Christ's teaching on salvation he says again and again that salvation is unmerited, but it is not unconditional. We may not be able say or do anything to earn our salvation, but we can say or do things that can put our salvation - and the salvation of others - in jeopardy. In fact, any- thing we say or do that puts the salvation of others at risk puts our own salvation at risk!

Jesus taught his disciples to pray for 'God's will to be done on earth as it is in heaven'.

Whenever they failed to do this, he taught them ask for forgiveness. That forgiveness was of course unmerited. Because, all forgiveness, by definition, is always unmerited. But the forgiveness, he taught them to ask for, was conditional, not unconditional. He taught them to say, 'Forgive us our sins, as we forgive those who have sinned against us'. And he lets his disciple know he means what he says. He tells them, 'For if you forgive people when they sin against you, your Heavenly Father will forgive you. But if you do not forgive people their sins, your Heavenly Father will not forgive your sins'.[7]

The point is obvious. And Christ repeats it in order to drive the point home. Grace can never, ever, be earned. But it is given to us on the condition that we give it to others.

When the disciples asked how often they were required to forgive someone, Jesus said, 'If your brother or sister sins, rebuke them, and if they repent, forgive them. If they sin against you seven times a day and seven times come back to you and say, "I repent," forgive them.[8]' And, on another occasion he said to the disciples, 'Actually, make that - not seven times - but seventy times seven!'[9]

The point is obvious. Because we have experienced grace we should extend grace. In this case - by extending forgiveness to others. And if others are to experience grace, they are to extend grace. In this case - by extending an apology to us. So it goes on - seventy times seven - or ad infinitum - until the whole world is full of the grace of God.

Jesus stressed the importance of this process to his disciples by telling them a parable. He said the Kingdom of Heaven on Earth is like a King who decided to settle accounts with his servants:

'A King wanted to settle accounts with his servants. When he began the process of settlement, a man who owed him millions of dollars was brought before him. When it was plain that he had no means of repaying the debt his master gave orders for the servant to be sold as a slave, along with his wife and his children, in order to repay at least some of his debt. At this the servant fell on his knees before his master. "Please be patient with me," he cried, "and I will pay you back every cent". Then the master, took pity on him, canceled his debt and set him free.
But when that servant went out, he found one of his fellow servants who owed him a few dollars. He grabbed him, seized him by the throat, saying, "Pay me what you owe me." At this his fellow servant fell at his feet and implored him, "Please be patient with me," he cried, "and I will

pay you back every cent". But he refused, and had his fellow servant put into prison until he repaid the debt.

When the other fellow servants saw what had happened, they were horrified And went and told their master everything that had happened. Then the master called the servant in. "You wicked servant!" he said. "Didn't I cancel your debt when you begged me to? Shouldn't you have taken pity on your fellow servant as I, your master, took pity on you?" In anger the master handed him over to the jailers until he repaid his debt.' [10]

When he had finished the story, Jesus turned to his disciples and pointedly said, 'This is how your Heavenly Father will treat you, unless you forgive your brother or your sister from your heart.'[11]

Note the same man who said, 'Father, forgive them, for they know not what they do,' is saying, 'unless you forgive your brother or your sister from your heart, your Heavenly Father will not forgive you'. He is saying that, forgiveness is offered freely to all. But it can only be ours if we give it to others in the same way that it has been given to us.

Just to be sure we've got the message correctly, let's just stay with the story a while, and unpack the narrative, piece by piece, as a parable of the process of salvation.

Was the servant who owed his master an unpayable debt doomed when it came to settling his account with the master? Yes. When the master decided to cancel his debt, was he saved? Yes. Was this salvation unmerited? Yes. Was this salvation unconditional? No. So what was the unwritten - but understood - condition of that salvation? That the servant would extend the same grace extended to him to his fellow servants.

The moral of the story is - salvation is about unmerited - but not unconditional - grace. It's about the cycle of alternately receiving and sharing God's grace 'from your heart'.

No Grace Without Sacrifice.

If we understand anything at all about grace we will not want to say or do anything that puts the salvation of others at risk, but we may be willing to put our own salvation at risk in order to save others. After all, the gospel is all about participating 'wholeheartedly' in the experience of extending God's amazing, but very risky grace, to the 'whole' world.

The protagonists of salvation in both testaments in the bible show they understood this very well. For example - take Moses - the 'greatest prophet' in the Old Testament; and - Paul - the 'greatest apostle' in the New Testament. Both Moses and Paul at times were actually prepared to put their own salvation at risk in order to try to save other people.

Moses came down from Mount Sinai, having received the Ten Commandments, only to find the people in open revolt, dancing round the idol of a Golden Calf that they had made to symbolize their rebellion against God. God was furious and threatened the people with punishment. Moses knew that God was furious. After all, he was furious with the people himself. But to save the people from destruction, Moses offered to try to intervene with God on their behalf. 'So Moses went to the Lord and said, "Oh, what a great sin these people have committed. They have made themselves gods of gold. But I beg you, please forgive them - if not, blot my name out of the book (of life) that you have written". God told Moses there was no way that he would punish the innocent on behalf of the guilty. But Moses was prepared to sacrifice his salvation to save others. [12]

Paul, as a Jew, was struggling with the implications of his people's rejection of Jesus as their Christ. 'Theirs are the patriarchs, theirs the covenants, theirs the promises', and 'theirs the human ancestry of Christ'. But Christ, he laments, is not theirs. Because they cut him down, and in the process they cut themselves off from him. 'I speak the truth in Christ', he says, 'I am not lying' when I say, 'I have great sorrow - unceasing anguish - in my heart' about the plight of the people of Israel. He says, 'For I could wish that I myself were cursed - cut off from Christ myself - for the sake of my brothers and sisters, those of my own race, the people of Israel,' - if it meant that they might be blessed. It seems Paul valued salvation so much that he couldn't stand by, holding on to his salvation, while the people he loved, lost it. He said he was 'not lying' when he said that he was more than willing to sacrifice his salvation to save others.[13]

In their willingness to sacrifice their safety and their security - even their salvation - in order to save others, Moses and Paul both point to the perfect sacrificial attitude that Jesus Christ displayed on the cross. 'Those who passed by ridiculed him, shaking their heads, hurling insults at him. "You saved others; but can you save yourself?" they cried. "Let the Christ, come down from the cross, that we may see and believe!" But he did not come down from the cross. And as a result many people lost faith in him. But whether they believed him, or not, Christ was willing to endure the cross. Not because he *could* not save himself; but because he *would* not save himself. He was more concerned about saving the people ridiculing him, than he was about saving himself. He did not come 'to be served, but to serve', and to sacrifice his life 'as a ransom for many'.[14]

When Jesus was asked about his willingness to sacrifice his life for others, he simply replied, 'I am the Good Shepherd. The Good Shepherd lays down his life for his sheep. The hired hand is not the shepherd who owns the sheep. So when he sees the wolf coming he runs away, abandoning the sheep. Then the wolf attacks the flock. The man runs away because he is a hired hand and cares nothing for the sheep. I am the Good Shepherd. I know my sheep, and my sheep know me. I lay down my life for my sheep. I lay it down of my own accord. For I am come that they might have life and have it to the full'.[15] And for Jesus, it seems, the matter of sacrifice was as straightforward as that.

The New Covenant.

At the Last Supper, the final meal Jesus had with his disciples before his execution, Jesus told the disciples about his understanding of the meaning of his crucifixion. He took the bread, broke it into pieces, and said, 'Take and eat. This is my body.' And he took the wine, poured it out for them, and said, 'Drink it, all of you. This my blood, the blood of the *new covenant*, which is poured out for many for the forgiveness of sins'.[16]

A *covenant* is a special relationship people commit themselves to. The *old covenant* was a special relationship that God entered into with the people of Israel.[17] It was a reciprocal agreement based on God's commitment to care for the people, and the people's commitment to cooperate with God. The terms of the agreement were outlined in the law.[18] If the people broke the law there was a provision for reconciliation based on the offering of a blood sacrifice with a penitent heart. The sacrifice was not required to appease the anger of God, but to remind the sinner of the awfulness of their sin in breaking their agreement. However these sacrifices proved to have real limitations in effecting real changes in people's hearts. 'The blood of goats sprinkled on those who are ceremonially unclean', made people outwardly, but not inwardly 'clean.'[19]

The *new covenant* was different from the *old covenant* in two important respects - one, it was recognized as being a relationship that was based on love rather than on law; and two, it was a relationship that was restored, not by any sacrifice we might make to God, but by the sacrifice that God, in Christ, made for us. And, of course, the hope was that the *new covenant*, written on our hearts, in 'the blood of Christ', would 'cleanse our consciences from acts that lead to death - to serve the living God!' [20]

For Paul the *new covenant* was the good news, and he encouraged us to celebrate the good news of the *new covenant* regularly at the Lord's Supper. 'Do this,' the Lord says, 'whenever you eat of this bread, and drink of this cup' in 'remembrance of me.' [21]

Now, one of the crucial questions that face us, is - what does this mean for us? What does it mean for us to 'do this' in 'remembrance of' Jesus today?

Carlos Christos, a Catholic from a middle class family in Brazil - who got involved as a lay brother working with the poor, and was put into prison for four years for his efforts - spent a period of time in prison trying to answer this question. In a letter from prison to his parents he wrote:

> 'Last year I meditated a great deal on the mystery of the Eucharist. Jesus instituted it in his last meal with his apostles, when he told them of the sufferings he would have to endure for their redemption. He took into his hands those most ordinary of foods, bread and wine, and he consecrated them. "This is my body which will be broken for you. This is my blood which will be shed for you. Do this in memory of me." What is the meaning of these words we repeat every mass? Do we simply mean that the consecration of the Mass is performed in memory of Jesus' sacrifice? No, they do not mean simply that. It is true that the Mass makes his sacrifice present here and now. But it also summons us to repeat Jesus' redemptive acts so we might be truly imitators of him. When the priest repeats the words in the Mass, "Do this in memory of me," I interpret it as Jesus saying to us: "I have loved you completely, so much that I willingly died for you. I've given all that I am to free you. Having nothing left but my life, I didn't grudge you that either. I gave it up to show you that the limits of love are to love without limits. I have

given you my body and my blood. I have made this gesture a sacrament so that at any time or place in human history you may receive it and re-enact it in your own life. When I said, 'Do this in memory of me,' I did not mean you should merely commemorate what I had done. I meant you should do likewise, that you should offer your body and blood for the redemption of humanity. Just as at the Mass you receive my body and blood, so in your lives you should offer up your own, so that my acts may always be present in the world through you." Unfortunately, many Christians do not realize that Mass is something to be lived rather than attended, and that it is to be lived to the extent that we are willing to sacrifice ourselves for the liberation of human beings, and so become *God's sacrament in the world.*'[22]

Now, this view that Carlos Christos advocates so eloquently in his letter - that we are called not only 'to receive' the sacrifice of Christ, but also 'to re-enact' the sacrifice of Christ, by 'repeating Jesus' redemptive acts in our own life' - has been the subject of great debate among Christians for centuries. And we cannot proceed further in our deliberations without considering arguments on both sides of this bitter-sweet dispute.

The Bitter-Sweet Dispute.

Martin Luther argued that, because our relationship was restored by the sacrifice that God made for us in Christ, we do not need to make any sacrifice. This doctrine, known as the doctrine of the *'Sweet Christ'*, asserts that Christ's final cry on the cross that 'it is finished' implies all the suffering required for salvation has already been accomplished. [23] Christ has done everything for us. There's nothing left for us to do. No more suffering is necessary. Anyone who 'mixes up' the necessity of Christ's suffering with the notion of Christians' suffering is attempting to attain their salvation through 'works' rather than 'grace'.[24] And, in so doing, is in danger of losing the *sweet* savor of Christ.

Thomas Muntzer argued that, because our relationship was restored by the sacrifice that God made for us in Christ, and we are called to be like Christ, we need to make sacrifices like Christ in order to restore others to a healthy relationship with God. This doctrine, known as the doctrine of the *'Bitter Christ'*, asserts that Christ 'completed' his suffering on the cross, but, as Paul says, we have to 'complete the sufferings of Christ' ourselves.[25] Christ may have done everything that was needed to do to save us. There may be nothing more that any of us need to do to save ourselves. But we still need to be prepared to suffer, to save others, like Christ did. It is not about anyone attempting to attain their salvation through 'works'; but it is about those of us who have already been saved by 'grace' sharing 'the grace of Christ' with others.[26] No doubt, suffering was a *bitter* experience for Christ, and suffering will be a *bitter* experience for us, but we are called to be like Christ, and we cannot be like Christ without suffering like Christ.

Needless to say many Christians through the centuries have opted for faith in a *Sweet Christ*, rather than face the obligation of following in the footsteps of the *Bitter Christ*.

Five hundred years ago Conrad Grebel wrote to Thomas Muntzer saying, ' today every (one) wants to be saved by a superficial faith - without love - without trial.'[27] And, five hundred years later, it is still pretty much the same. Today we are surrounded on every side by what Dorothee Soelle calls 'Bourgeois Christianity' - 'suffering-free Christianity'. Which, she says, is not totally without suffering; but 'leaves the suffering to others'. [28]

Jakob Kautz wrote to the Christians of his day who, in his view, had subscribed to faith 'without love' and 'without trial', reminding them that, 'Jesus Christ did not suffer for us in any other way than this: that we should walk in his footsteps in the way that he blazed for us.'[29] While in our day, people like Simone Weil remind us that Christianity without suffering is an illusion. After all, she says, 'even the risen Christ still ha(s) his scars.'[30]

But nobody in the twentieth century enjoined the debate, about which way Christians ought to go, more vigorously than the famous German theologian Dietrich Bonhoeffer. Bonhoeffer insisted that the debate was not an argument about 'works' versus 'grace', but about two mutually exclusive views of 'grace'. Bonhoeffer characterized the option presented by the *Sweet Christ* as 'cheap grace', and the option presented by the *Bitter Christ* as 'costly grace'. He said that 'cheap grace' is 'grace without a price'; a 'doctrine about the Love of God without the incarnation of the Word of God'. He said that 'cheap grace is grace without discipleship, grace without the cross, grace without Jesus Christ, living and incarnate'. And he said that 'cheap grace' was the ruin of Christianity. So Bon- hoeffer said he was going to fight for 'costly grace', that not only preached the grace of Christ, but also practiced the grace of Christ, even if it was going to cost him his life.[31]

The New Commandment.

When we reflect on these views in the light of scripture it is clear that the point Carlos Christos makes is correct. We are called not only 'to receive' the sacrifice of Christ, but also 'to re-enact' the sacrifice of Christ, by 'repeating his redemptive acts in our own life'.

Jesus instituted his *new covenant* with a *new commandment*. The *old* commandment had been: that you 'love your neighbour as you love yourself'.[32] But Jesus said, 'A *new* commandment I give to you: that you love one another as I have loved you!'[33] Now the big difference that there is between the *old commandment* and the *new commandment* is simply the way in which we are called to love one another. In the *old* covenant we are expected to '*love our neighbour as we have loved ourselves*'. But in the *new* covenant we are expected to '*love our neighbour as Christ has loved us*'. It is loving one another, '*as Christ has loved us*', that is the quintessential characteristic of the *new covenant* that Christ inaugurated on the cross.

Note that the new commandment is about loving, not about suffering. We are called to love, not to suffer. But, if suffering is necessary to do justice in the face of injustice, then so be it; the call to love, in that case, is a call for us to suffer for others in the same way as Christ suffered for us. 'Christ suffered for you', Peter wrote, 'leaving you an *example* - that you might follow in his footsteps!'[34] The telling word in that sentence is the word Peter used in his letter for *example*. It is *hupogrammos*. Which designates the perfect line of writing at the top of an exercise book, that anyone who wants to learn to write, needs to learn to copy, as closely as they can. So Peter is saying that 'we need to copy

Christ as closely as we can when it comes to developing our capacity to suffer for the sake of love'.[35] And Muntzer and Bonhoeffer and Soelle and Weil would sign off on that.

In his Epistle to the Philippians Paul unpacks the implications of Christ's example for us:

> '*Each of you should not look to your own interests, but also to the interests of others. You should have exactly the same attitude as*

Christ Jesus had:
   "For he who had always been God by nature,
   did not cling to his prerogatives as God's equal,
   But he stripped himself of all privilege,
   emptied himself, and made himself nothing,
   in order to be born by nature as a mortal.
   And, having become a human being,
   he humbled himself,
   living the life of a slave,
   a life of utter obedience, even unto death.
   And the death he died, on the cross,
   was the death of a common criminal".[36]

This is an extraordinary exhortation to a degree of self-forgetful sacrificial love that staggers the imagination of most ordinary mortals. And yet Paul seems to expect that people, like you and me, can incarnate exactly the same attitude as Christ Jesus had.

He expects us to empty ourselves of our own preoccupations and make more time and space for others. He expects us empathize with others and join them in their struggle to love and be loved. And he expects us empower others and support them in their quest to live their lives to the full - even if it kills us.

The Spirit Of Christ.

TEAR Australia is sensitive to criticism that sincere non-Christians, like Gandhi, have made about Christians preaching grace, but not practicing it. Like Bonhoeffer, we feel called to practice grace, not 'cheap grace', but 'costly grace', personally and politically. We have no illusions about the disdain with which many 'sweet' Christians, whom we know, treat the 'bitter' call to practice what we preach. But nevertheless, we, in TEAR Australia, still seek to encourage Aussie Christians to develop a life of sacrificial love, so as to reflect the love of Christ more faithfully in the context of our suffering world.

We constantly *articulate* the necessity for Aussie Christians to 'put love into action'. In fact, for many years, TEAR Australia's by-line in its publications was 'love in action'. On the cover of *Target* Number One for the Year Two Thousand the line was still the same. 'And what does the Lord require of you?' it asks. 'To act justly, and to love mercy, and to walk humbly with your God!' it cries aloud to its readers in bold black and white type.[37]

We constantly *cultivate* the priority of Aussie Christians 'putting love into action' by get-ting people to reflect on their response to global suffering in the light of the gospel itself.

Every *Target* magazine has a Bible Study, and every Bible Study gets people to read passages that remind us that: 'God is love. Whoever lives in love lives in God, and God lives in them. Whoever loves, knows God. Whoever does not love, does not know God. For God is love. This is love: not that we loved God, but that he loved us. This is how we know what love is: Jesus Christ laid down his life for us. And we ought to lay down our lives for one another. If anyone is well to do and sees someone in want and shuts their eyes - and their heart - how can anyone believe the love of God lives in them? Let us love, not merely in theory, as policy, but in sincerity and in reality - in truth.'[38]

We constantly *illustrate* the possibility of Aussie Christians 'putting love into action', by telling stories about how other Christians from other countries around the world are 'putting love into action'. One of our favourite stories is about Dagoretti Corner Baptist Church. It has been featured in *Target* a couple of times recently. The first time in 1997, and the second time in 1999. For us, Dagoretti Corner Baptist Church has been a great example of how a church can be 'compelling proof of the love of God' in a community.

> 'Confronted by the poverty of opportunity in the shambas (small holdings) and small towns of rural Kenya some have been lured by the false promise of the big city. Others, despairing of the bloody conflict in southern Sudan ever ending, have sought sanctuary in the comparative peace of this Nairobi slum. Comparative, because sudden eruptions of violence, a sad consequence of stress, and illicit alcohol, are all too frequent in the narrow alleyways and muddy compounds of this cor-rugated iron comrnunity of squatters. Whatever their reason for being there, most of those who live in Dagoretti Corner do all within their power to raise their kids safely, and work for a better future.
> But it is tough, very tough.
>
> For the low-skilled and poorly-qualified paid work is very difficult to acquire, legitimate full-time employment, almost impossible. As a result

most earn less than $US I a day, which leaves them well below the official poverty line.

Some adults, mostly male, whether driven by despair or less constrained by strong principles, flee the responsibilities they feel unable to carry, and abandon both children and partner. Despite the epidemic levels of HIV/AIDS, some women resort to prostitution as one of the few ways available to earn what they need to provide for themselves and their children. Others join the ranks of those who brew changaa, a potent and illegal maize-based liquor which sells well because of the temporary relief from pain it offers to its consumers.

Just over twelve years ago the Rev. William Eyika, began with his wife Grace the work of planting a church in this apparently God-forsaken corner of Nairobi. But like many others involved in similar programs in equally impoverished communities, their very presence indicates the depth of God's concern for the poor. Dagoretti Corner Baptist Church is compelling proof of the love of God.

In 1988 the church formed the Dagoretti Corner Self-Help Group (SHG), and under the supervision of this group a wide range of developmental and relief responses are being made to the needs of this very poor community. The coordinators of these programs are all people from the local community, many of whom have come to faith, and found new hope and direction through the church's ministries.

School fees and associated costs (uniforms. books etc) place primary schooling beyond the reach of most families in the Dagoretti Corner community, and thosewho miss out on formal education are almost inevitably condemned to a life of poverty. It's a vicious, self-perpetuating cycle. The SHG Primary School, housed in the church building, is an effective means of breaking this cycle. With only 15 staff and very limited resources and more than 660 kids crowded into flimsily-partitioned classrooms, conditions are far from ideal. But there is no doubting the dedication of the teachers. And the outcomes are very significant.

Last year all 25 students who sat the end-of-primary-school exams passed, and were able to gain entry into either high schools or vocational training institutions. The realization that such an achievement opens up the real possibility of a different and more prosperous future is clearly expressed in this letter written to the Headmaster by Caroline Mutola, 6 months after she graduated from the school.

"I joined Dagoretti Corner Primary School in 1995 in Standard 6. Although life was good in Standard 6 I faced several problems, especially in some subjects which I could not understand easily. I worked very hard, after some time I began to understand the subject matter. I even started writing and reading well, as the teachers were strict but friendly. The school provided textbooks, and past papers for revision in Standard 8. There were also storybooks, maps, blackboards etc which made the education enjoyable. There were also sports and games, which I loved very much. I plan to be a nurse in future, when I finish my education, and become self-employed in my clinic, get married and have beautiful children."

Another important development component of the SHG's program is in vocational training projects. Over the last 12 years nearly a 1000 students have completed courses in motor mechanics, carpentry or tailoring. Most of these students have moved to other parts of the city or country, and so it is impossible to obtain a comprehensive picture of how effective these courses are in helping the graduates obtain long-term employment.

However; an evaluation done of the 1988-98 period of those former students who could be located was most encouraging. 133 graduates were surveyed. Their average annual income before training was less than $26 a year, compared to $222 since graduation.

Beatrice Atieno is a young single graduate of the 1996 tailoring class. Since graduating, she has gained employment in the Kawangare market where her sewing earns her $56 per month. Susan Wamitha has now established her own sewing business and is earning $130 per month, which helps her provide for 3 other dependents.

These programs, together with a health care project and a women's self-help micro-enterprise project, are a remarkably comprehensive response to the very great needs of the people who live in the Dagoretti Corner slum. Moreover, a childhood and early child-hood intervention project is extending the compassionate work of Dagoretti Corner Baptist Church into several neighbouring slum communities.

When the members and staff of Dagoretti Comer Baptist Church talk to their neighbours about the gospel, the good news of God's love for the poor, their actions show that they know what they are talking about. There is an on-going invasion of grace in the neighbourhood, and many women and men can testify to the power of God's love to change their lives.'[39]

We constantly *demonstrate* the practicality of Aussie Christians 'putting love into action', by showing how Christians are 'putting love into action' in our own backyard in the same way that Christians are 'putting love into action' overseas. Donna Mulhearn, was a TEAR rep. at Maitland Baptist Church, who returned home after visiting our TEAR partners at Dagoretti Corner Baptist Church, wondering how Christians could do the same kind of community work, in Australia, as she saw in Africa. So Donna came to do a course we call, 'With Christ in the Community', that we run in Brisbane twice a year. Lyn and Steve Hatfield-Dodds, describe what the course was like:

'The course ran for an intensive two and a half weeks, and included studies on Christ's life, input from a wide range of people, and practical experience being in the neighbourhood.

The daily program started around 6.30 am with prayer - experimenting with new ways of encountering Christ, and getting a feel for what it might be like to work with him in the local community. After breakfast we joined in studies drawn from the gospels, focusing on Christ, and what it means for us to become more Christ-like.

In the latter part of the morning (people) shared of their life in the local community - involved in peace networks, community arts, housing assistance, legal aid, refugee resettlement, and offering hospitality and shelter to those without a place to stay.

The afternoons were unstructured times, to allow us to get to know the neigh-bourhood, and its people. In the evenings we had dinner with different members of the network. Most days finished with a much-needed briefing session. We also managed to squeeze in time to deliver meals on wheels, go on outings (with people who were intellectually disabled), and help out at an evening meal for over a hundred homeless men.

The nine of us on the course lived in a group house for the first week, moving out to stay in boarding houses or hostels we found for ourselves in the second week. For many of us this was a difficult and sometimes frightening experience, living in the midst of depressed and often violent lives, and it was good to come back together for the last few days to the security of group living.

Highlights of the course for us (included) being involved in a Murri service in a maximum security prison; hearing people's stories; developing friendships; (and) meeting people who not only talk about being Christ-like or compassionate, but who are trying to put these things into practice. '[40]

After the course Donna went on to become a part of the "human shield" movement. The "human shield" movement is a term 'describing the deliberate location of civilians in or around combat targets to deter an enemy from attacking those targets.' In January 2003 Donna and a group of dedicated anti-war activists set out for Iraq to act as "human shields", protecting vulnerable essential civilian sites and services from the potentially catastrophic impact of the impending "shock and awe campaign".

Some "human shields" were placed at the 'Al Daura Electrical Plant, Baghdad South Electrical Plant, 7 April Water Treatment Plant, Al Daura Water Treatment Plant, Tejio Food Silo, Al Daura Oil Refinery and Al Mamun Telecommunications Facility'. Others decided to base themselves in schools, hospitals, and orphanages. A list of these deployments were 'sent to the Joint Chiefs of Staff together with a request that they recognize their assertion that targeting these sites would be in violation of Article 54 Protocol Additional to the Geneva Convention. There was no response to the letters'. But 'none of the 80 shields who stayed in Baghdad throughout the war were killed or injured'. And 'none of the sites where they were residing were destroyed.'[41]

Donna later returned as a humanitarian aid worker to set up a shelter for street kids in Baghdad and assist homeless families. During this she survived constant bombing, being kidnapped by fighters and shot at by American soldiers. 'In order to undertake aid work in Iraq, a group of former "human shields", including Donna, established 'Our Home – Iraq' as an independent organisation designed to carry out projects to assist children and families affected by the war. Its work has included setting up a shelter for street-kids in Baghdad and a centre for traumatised children. It is now supporting projects to assist refugee families made homeless by the war.'

In *Ordinary Courage* Donna says she 'is motivated by the tradition of non-violent action, and inspired by the radical Christian teaching of non-violence as a way of life. Donna's inspiration to join the "human shields" was the Christ of St Francis of Assisi: "*Lord, make me an instrument of your peace, where there is hatred, let me bring love...*" [42]

My wife, Ange, says the call of Christ is clear. Christ calls us to practice 'a life of sacrifice'. We may not hear the call. We may not want to hear the call. But the call, she insists, remains the same today as it always was: 'If anyone would come after me,' Christ says, 'let them deny themselves, take up their cross, daily, and follow me. Whoever wants to save their life will lose it, but whoever loses their life, for me, will save it.' [43]

There's probably no better way for me to conclude this series of meditations than to leave you with an excerpt from Ange's well-known poem,

'Who Of You Will Join Me?'

'There is precious little acceptance in our society
of the changes in our bodies
brought about by sacrifice,
by the giving of life to others.
People want us to look
unscathed, unscarred;
without the sagging in our breasts;
the stretchmarks on our stomach;
the lines of strain and struggle.
Where is the place for the beauty, derived from love,
and developed through sacrifice?
Where are the people who will celebrate
the signs of someone who has given themselves to others
through touch in tears with love unnumbered times?
Who of you will join me
in forsaking the images we idolize in our society?
Who of you will join me
in turning away from the mirror towards the door
that leads to the needs of others?
Who of you will join me
of being wrinkled,
We are not fools
who give what we cannot keep, to gain what we cannot lose!' [44]

In The Footsteps Of Christ - A Consecration

We stare at the cross, and hear you say:
'Take up your cross and follow me.'
We tremble with fear; we pale with shame;
Its not the way we thought it would be.

'This is my body that is broken for you.'
'This is my blood that was shed.'
'This is my prayer: that you do this too,
For others, in remembrance of me.'

There is no salvation,
If there is no grace.
There is no grace, if no sacrifice.
There is no laughter,
If we do not cry.
There is no life, if we do not die.

There's no other way to prove your love,
But to give, as we have been given.
There's no other way to prove your love,
But forgive, as we've been forgiven.

There is no salvation,
If there is no grace.
There is no grace, if no sacrifice.
There is no laughter,
If we do not cry.
There is no life, if we do not die.

There's no other way to prove your love,
But to try our best to the end.
There's no other way to prove your love,
But lay down our lives for our friends.
There's no other way but redemption.
There's no other way but prayer.
There's no other way but compassion.
There's no other way but care.
There's no other way but religion.

There's no other way but love.
There's no other way but sacrifice.
There's no other way but the cross.

Download lyrics, music and mp3 of "The Way Of Christ" free from
http://www.daveandrews.com.au/songs/10_the_way_of_christ.mp3

Ideas For Meditation, Discussion and Action.

1. Why do people react to Christians saying: 'we're not perfect - just forgiven?'

2. How do you understand the theological concept of 'salvation by grace'?

3. What conditions, if any, are stipulated for people to be 'saved by grace'?

4. Why do you think that Moses, Jesus, and Paul were all prepared to sacrifice their salvation for the sake of others?

5. How is the new covenant different from the old covenant?

6. How is the new commandment different from the old commandment?

7. What difference, if any, does it make whether people believe in 'cheap grace' or in 'costly grace'?

8. Why is the by-line 'love in action' so significant for a Christian agency?

9. How does TEAR encourage Aussie Christians to 'put love into action'?

10. What do you need to do to 'put love into action' more in your life?

An Important Postscript On The Cross As A Strategy In The Struggle For Transformation.

Stanley Jones, the famous American missionary to India in the mid-twentieth century, says that Christians have a Hindu to thank for 'putting the cross back into politics'.[45] It was Mahatma Gandhi, a Hindu, who, undeterred by debates about the deity of Christ, rediscovered the humanity of Christ, and in so doing, recovered the story of the cross as a crucial strategy for ordinary humans to use in their ongoing fight for good against evil.

Gandhi said 'The gentle figure of Christ - so patient, so kind, so loving, so full of forgive-ness that he taught his followers not to retaliate when struck, but to turn the other cheek - was a beautiful example of the perfect person'.[46] Christ, the 'martyr, was an embodiment of sacrifice', and the cross 'a great example of suffering'.[47] 'Jesus lost his life on the cross'. But Jesus didn't lose the battle. 'Jesus won. As the world's history has abundantly shown'. And, consequently, 'the example of Christ' is a crucial 'factor in the composition of my underlying faith in nonviolence - which rules all my actions.' [48]

Gandhi said, 'the art of true self-defense - by which man gains his life by losing it - has not (yet) been perfected for application by large masses of mankind'. *'Satyagraha'* - his famous experiment with 'truth-force' in the struggle for independence - was, he said, 'an experiment in that direction'.[49]

During the struggle for independence in India, Gandhi developed a 'code of conduct', 'rules for engagement', and 'stages of a campaign' for those who wanted to be committed to a strategy of Christ-like nonviolent resistance to the politics of oppression.

The code of conduct, laid down by Gandhi in 1930, included the following requirements:

1. Never harbor any anger, but suffer the anger of an opponent.

2. Do not submit to an order given in anger, even if threatened.

3. Refuse to return assaults.

4. Refrain from insults.

5. Protect opponents from insult or attack, even at the risk of life.

6. Do not resist arrest.

7. If taken prisoner, behave in an exemplary manner.[50]

The rules of engagement - outlined by Gandhi - were elaborated by Bose, as follows:

1. There must be self-reliance at all times. Outside help may be used in the engagement, but not as a substitute for personal responsibility.

2. Engagement should be proactive, not reactive. Constantly monitoring the engagement to make sure that the actions are always constructive.

3. Education of the public, the participants, and the opponent, in the art of constructive action are an integral part of the process of engagement.

4. Any demands for changes that are made, must be reasonable requests. Not the maximum, but the minimum demands, consistent with the truth.

5. The opponent should not be expected to make any more changes than the participants are prepared to make in the resolution of their conflict.

6. If the opponent is unwilling to change, participants should be willing to move slowly, but surely, into the successive stages of a campaign.

7. There should be a persistent search to find a peaceful settlement at every stage of the campaign - to destroy the enmity - not the enemy.

8. In working out a settlement, participants need to cooperate with their opponents as much as they can, without compromising their principles.[51]

And the stages of a campaign - developed by Gandhi - are listed by Shridharani:

9. Negotiation. Every effort must be made to redress a grievance, or resolve a conflict through the established channels for mediation and arbitration.

10. Preparation. If mediation and arbitration fails, then participants need to prepare themselves, through prayer -and fasting - to take direct action.

11. Agitation. Direct action takes many forms - from meetings to marches - but all of the many forms of direct action need to be strictly nonviolent.

12. Presentation. If there is no response, the opponent should be presented with a serious proposal; and an ultimatum, if no response is forthcoming.

13. Demonstration. The participants need to demonstrate their commitment to the cause, where appropriate, by public boycotts and general strikes.

14. Non-cooperation. Depending upon the issues involved, non-cooperation might involve either nonpayment of taxes - or noncompliance with a law.

15. Civil Disobedience. Noncompliance with a law involves civil disobedience. Laws should only be disobeyed if central to, or symbolic of, the grievance.

16. Parallel Governance. If the grievances are still not addressed, then the participants should assume responsibility to deal with them themselves.[52]

Now, it seems to me, seldom, if ever, has anyone enunciated a more Christ-like set of principles for conducting a campaign of nonviolent resistance to political oppression than Gandhi did when he laid out his 'code of conduct', 'rules for engagement', and 'stages of a campaign'. And we would be well advised as Christians, to follow the lead of our Hindu guide in this regard, if we would want to follow in the footsteps of Christ.

Gandhi was once heard to say, 'Given a just cause, a capacity for endless suffering, and the avoidance of violence,' through *satyagraha*, 'victory is certain!'[53] Certainly, through *satyagraha* Gandhi challenged the largest Empire the world had ever known, shook it to its very foundations, and contributed to its final collapse as a global power. And, since Gandhi, everyone from Martin Luther King to Desmond Tutu - and Aung San Suu Kyi - have used *satyagraha* as a strategy to engage oppression, and to struggle for liberation, in a completely resolute, consistently nonviolent, incredibly sacrificial fashion.

However, with the last century being as preoccupied, as it was with technology, people tended to play around with *satyagraha* as a technique. Some rejected it as a technique - for being 'too inefficient'; others rejigged it as a technique - to make it 'more efficient'.

Satyagraha was considered to be 'too inefficient' as an instrument for transformation because it was a slow process, rather than a quick fix - and it presupposed a unfashion-able willingness to suffer for the sake of others.

Attempts to make *satyagraha* 'more efficient', did so by taking the strategy out of the context of the story of the cross - making it less dependent upon the power of the Spirit, and more dependent upon people's own capacity to save themselves.

But if the story of the cross is about anything, it is about the fact that we cannot save ourselves; that it is an illusion to believe we can save the world - apart from the Spirit.

We may develop the knowledge to save, but without the Spirit, personified in Christ on the cross, we tend to utilize our skills to save some - not all - ourselves, not others.

Gandhi recognized the danger of this possibility when he stated quite categorically that the use of the strategy of *satyagraha*, without the spirit of *satyagraha*, was not really *satyagraha* at all - but what he called *'duragraha'* or 'self-centred stubbornness'.[54]

Attempts to make the strategy of the cross 'more efficient', by taking it out of the context of the story of the cross, only serve to make it 'less effective' as an instrument of salvation. Without the spirit of grace, the technique of *satyagraha* itself becomes a dis-grace.

Thus Gandhi calls on all those who care about transformation on the international scene to remember not only the strategy of Christ on the cross, but also the Spirit personified in the story of Christ on the cross. Over and over again Gandhi reminds us that *'nations can only be made (and remade) through the agony of the cross - and no other way!'*[55]

However, those of us who choose to embrace the way of the cross, because there is *'no other way'*, would do well to bear in mind that the cross - in and of itself - is a dead end. We may indeed to be willing to lay down our lives for others, like Christ did on the cross, but without the power that raised Christ from the dead, there is simply no way forward from that point on. *The cross only becomes the way forward through the resurrection.*

The Apostle Paul concedes: 'If there is no resurrection of the dead, then not even Christ has been raised. And if Christ has not been raised, your faith is futile'. And those who die for Christ 'are lost'. If 'only for this life we have hope in Christ, we are to be pitied'. [56]

Is it any wonder, therefore, that Paul confides to his friends: 'I want to know Christ and the power of his resurrection.'[57] He says, for 'if we were reconciled through the death' of Christ, 'how much more, having been reconciled, shall we be saved through his life!' [58] He says 'I want to know the fellowship of sharing in his sufferings, becoming like him in his death, and so, somehow, to attain to the resurrection from the dead'. [59]

'Praise be to the God of our Lord Jesus Christ!' cries the Apostle Peter. 'For in his great mercy he has given us …a living hope through the resurrection of Jesus Christ from the dead'. 'In this', he says, 'you (can) greatly rejoice, though now for a little while you may have to suffer grief in all kinds of trials'. These 'trials have come', he says, 'so that your faith - of greater worth than gold, which perishes even though refined by fire - may be proved genuine and may result in glory when Jesus Christ is revealed!'[60]

So it is that we are called to embrace the way of the cross as the way we are to engage the world; not trusting in the cross itself but in the One who calls us to take up the cross; for it is only the once-crucified, now-resurrected Christ, who can take us by the hand and lead us from death to life, through the pain of crucifixion and the hope-against-hope of resurrection, that the way of the cross inevitably entails for all who would embrace it.

Notes

1   M.Gandhi *An Autobiography* The Navjivan Press Ahmedabad 1927 p90-92
2   Rom.6:15,13
3   1John1:7,9
4   Heb.9:13
5   Heb.9:14
6   Heb.10:26-29
7   Math.6:10,12,14-15
8   Luke17:3-4
9   Math.18:21-22
10   Math.18:23-34
11   Math.18:35
12   Exod.32:31-32
13   Rom.9:1-5
14   Math.20:25,28
15   John10:14,11-13,15,10
16   Math.26:26-28
17   Exod.24:1-8
18   Exod.24:7
19   Heb.9:13
20   Heb.9:14
21   1 Cor.11:23-27
22   C.Christos *Letters From A Prisoner Of Conscience*. Lutterworth Press London 1978 p15-16
23   John19:30
24   M.Luther *Luthers Werke in Auswahl*, De Gruyter Berlin 1950 Vol.7 p102-103
25   Col.1:24
26   Eph.2:1-10
27   T.Lorenzen 'Acting In Hope'. *Hearing The Cry- Acting In Hope*. Melbourne 2000 p3
28   D.Soelle ibid p130
29   T.Lorenzen ibid p3
30   D.Soelle ibid p155
31   D.Bonhoeffer *The Cost Of Discipleship* MacMillan New York 1963 pp45-47
32   Lev.19:18
33   John13:34
34   1Pet.2:21
35   W.Barclay ibid p95
36   Phil.2:1-8
37   *Target* No.1 2000 Cover
38   1John 4:18,7-10; 3:16-18
39   'God-forsaken?' *Target* No.4 1999 p12-16
40   L.&S. Dodds 'Redeeming our Passion - Renewing Our Dream'. *Target* No.2 1992 p22-23
41   http://en.wikipedia.org/wiki/Human_shield_action_to_Iraq
42   http://www.pilgrimstoryteller.com

43	John 15:12-15
44	A.Andrews in D. Andrews *Building A Better World* Albatross Sutherland 1996 p203-204
45	S.Jones *Christ Of The Indian Road* Hodder & Stoughton London 1927 p88
46	Gandhi, M. *The Message Of Jesus,*: Bharitya Vidya Bhavan Bombay 1971 foreword
47	Ibid., 7
48	Ibid., 7
49	M.Gandhi *The Science Of Satyagraha* Bharatiya Vidya Bhavan Bombay 1970 p129
50	D.Tendulkar *Mahatma* Vol.III Jhaveri and Tendulkar, Bombay 1952 p17
51	N. Bose *Studies in Gandhism* Indian Associated Publishing Calcutta 1947 p175
52	K.Shridharani *War Without Violence* Harcourt, Brace New York 1939 pp5-42
53	M.Gandhi *Nonviolence In Peace And War* Vol.II, p64
54	J.Bondurant *Conquest Of Violence* University Of California Press Berkeley 1958 p41-44
55	M.Gandhi *The Message Of Jesus Christ* Bharatiya Vidya Bhavan Bombay 1971 p68
56	I Cor.15:13-18(edited)
57	Phil.3:10
58	Rom.5:10
59	Phil.3:10
60	1 Pet.1:3-7(edited)